Shaping the Skyline

The World According to Real Estate Visionary Julien Studley

PETER HELLMAN

John Wiley & Sons, Inc.

Published by John Wiley & Sons, Inc., Hoboken, New Jersey.
Published simultaneously in Canada.

Library of Congress Cataloging-in-Publication Data

Hellman, Peter, 1943-
Shaping the skyline: the world according to real estate visionary Julien Studley / Peter Hellman.
p. cm.
Includes index.
ISBN 0-471-65766-2 (cloth)
1. Studley Inc.—History. 2. Studley, Julien J. 3. Real estate agents—New York (State)—New York—Biography. I. Title.
HD277.J85H46 2004
333.33′092—dc22

2004003668

Printed in the United States of America

10 9 8 7 6 5 4 3 2 1

Contents

Foreword

By Bob Kerrey

Julien and I became friends in 1999 when I was serving in the United States Senate. He introduced himself after I spoke to a business and education task force on which he was serving. During the time I was preparing myself for a re-election campaign Julien called to ask me if I would help him think of some unconventional candidates to lead a university in New York City called the New School. I had never heard of the school, but after he gave me some details, I did as he asked.

Then, for the next few days I couldn't shake the idea that maybe Julien was thinking about me for this position. When I called to ask, he said he was but he wanted me to reach that conclusion first. That is Julien at his poker-playing best. He waited for me to play my hand and at that point the game was over. Today, I am leading the university that is Julien's higher education love.

The story of Julien Studley's half century of business success is an especially moving example of an immigrant who used the freedom of his adopted nation to great benefit. But this is also the story of the bloody twentieth century, a traumatic era that comes into focus when the details of Julien's life are learned.

Julien was 12 years old and living safely with his family in Brussels, Belgium, on September 1, 1939, when Germany invaded Poland, provoking a declaration of war by France and England. The Armistice, which signaled the end of the Great War on November 11, 1918, and the peace treaty of Versailles that was completed the following summer, became little more than a two-decade-long interruption in the fighting, a word we use too often to describe a horror too terrible to face directly.

Residents of Brussels, who remembered the Great War had begun with the German invasion of Belgium in August 1914, were not complacent. They knew that odds favored a second such attack. With the German army massed and preparing for the assault that began on May 10, 1940, and ended 18 days later with the French and English retreating to Dunkirk, France, Julien's family moved to the relative safety of Nice, France.

For Americans, whose historical myth includes the unqualified rescue of Europe during the Second World War, Julien's life is an unpleasant reminder that we almost waited too long. That fall, as the German army continued its march into France a presidential election was taking place in the United States. And both of our candidates for President,

Franklin Delano Roosevelt and Wendell Wilkie, were strongly opposed to the United States breaking its neutrality.

After the election President Roosevelt, with Wilkie's strong support, began the Lend-Lease program that gave England a chance to successfully defend itself. However, it was not enough to save Julien's family. In 1941 the Nazi danger sent them to flee once more. This time they went to Cuba because they could not get a visa to the United States. Our neutrality did not end until the day after the December 7th Japanese attack on Pearl Harbor, when Germany declared war on us.

The Studleys came to New York in 1943. He became interested in real estate almost immediately, credits the New School for giving him his education, joined the Army where an association with men who had graduated from all the best schools gave him confidence he could succeed against all competition, and started Studley Real Estate in 1954. Fifty years later the name has become a trademark denoting quality, integrity, and service.

What he built and did during that time is the subject of this book. So, too, is the way that he did it. Julien Studley has never forgotten to be grateful. Somewhere he learned that the best decisions are made after listening to everyone else speak instead of making everyone listen to you. Somehow, he has managed to be guided by two apparently incompatible habits: the energetic determination to finish what he starts and the outwardly calm demeanor of an expert poker player.

Julien Studley never misplaced his curiosity in the lives of others nor does he conveniently reduce life to the numerical necessity of an actuary. "How are you doing?" is among his favorite questions, in a manner and mood that lets you know this is not a perfunctory interrogation. It is in the answer to this question that Julien keeps rediscovering a good reason for optimism and hope.

Biographical Note on Bob Kerrey

Prior to becoming president of the New School University in 2001, Bob Kerrey represented Nebraska for 12 years in the United States Senate. Before that, he served as Nebraska's governor for four years. In February 2004, Kerrey was appointed by Tom Daschle to a bipartisan commission charged with studying the intelligence failures that preceded the attacks of 9/11.

Educated in pharmacy at the University of Nebraska, Bob Kerrey served three years in the United States Navy during the Vietnam War. He was awarded the Congressional Medal of Honor. He is the author of *When I Was a Young Man: A Memoir,* published in 2000 by Harcourt Books. Kerrey is married to Sarah Paley. The couple have a young son, Henry, who was born September 10, 2001. Kerrey's children from a previous marriage are named Ben and Lindsey.

Acknowledgments

One aim of this book is to bring the reader down to where the action is as real estate deals are stalked, negotiated, and closed. In that effort, I've depended on the willingness of current and former Studley brokers to be interviewed and reinterviewed. I am grateful to Mitch Steir, Michael Colacino, Peter Capuciati, Mike Solomon, Rick Marek, Joe Learner, Laurie Condon, John Goodman, Paul Revson, Art Greenberg, Mark Jaccom, Ted Rotante, Lois Zambo, Steve Goldstein, Seth Dudley, John Conerty, Julie Schuelke, Bill Quinby, Scott Pannick, Peter Speier, Jacque Ducharme, Rick Schuham, Stan Kovak, Paul Schweitzer, David Raspler, Emil Schattner, Steve Grill, Charles McArthur, and Matthew Purser. Extra gratitude goes to Kurt Handschumacher in New York and Howard Sadowsky in Los Angeles. Nick Borg, formerly the company's chief operating officer, adroitly sketched in the big picture.

When I needed information about particular deals, some completed decades ago, research wunderkind Alexandria Faiz always came through, no matter how busy she happened to be. On the administrative side, Marion Kennedy, Shelonda Mason, Tommy Chu, Wendy Zhang, Tsun Tam, Margaret Luberda, Alicia Godfrey, Karen Hickey, and Lisa Walker were kind to me in many ways. Andy Seidmen's reading of the manuscript made me appreciate lawyer precision.

More help in fleshing out the deals came from Fred H. Hill, the late Jack Freidin, Mel Juffe, Jerry Speyer, Charles Overby, Jimmy Thomas, Barry Traub, Tom Webler, and Peter Bourbeau, and Matt Bialecki. For background on Julien's work on the boards of public institutions, I thank Bob Kerrey and Jim Murtha at New School University, Rebecca Robertson at Lincoln Center for the Performing Arts, and Frances Degen Horowitz at the Graduate Center of City University. Early encouragement for this book came from Henry Wollman, director of the Steven L. Newman Real Estate Institute at Baruch College. Thanks, too, to Carolyn Dunn at The Durst Library of The Real Estate Board of New York. And to master accountant Nate Gordon.

For their willingness to be interviewed about the destruction of the downtown office at the World Trade Center, I am grateful to Jill Gartenberg and Kevin Puma, each of whom suffered the loss of a spouse on 9/11. Even now, as I think of their courage in getting on with life with small children, my heart is pierced. Thanks also to Robert Goodman and especially to Barbara Kennish, best friend of Patricia Puma.

My first contact with the company called Studley was initiated by Gerald Freeman, that rare press agent who always put the needs of the journalist, and ultimately the reader, ahead of those of the client. In 1974, Gerry introduced me to Don Schnabel, the company's vice chairman. Decades later, Don kept me on course as I tried to understand Studley.

George Studley and Irene Melup filled me in on many details of Studley history, as did Ivar Stackgold and Joseph Rykwert. Serge Klarsfeld uncovered documentation concerning the family's sojourn in France during the Nazi Occupation. Mel Juffe and Norm Rappaport filled in details of life with Julien in the army.

A manuscript is only that. Mine became a book thanks to the superb efforts of agent Linda Konner, executive editor Debra Englander, and senior production editor Michael Lisk.

Finally, I owe thanks to Julien Studley. He shared freely with me his strong ideas about business and leadership. But if Julien also had strong ideas about how this book should be shaped, and he probably did, he kept them to himself so that I could feel free to go my own way. It is always a treat to be with him.

Introduction

In the fall of 1968, at age 25, I came to the big city from Falls Church, Virginia, to be an apprentice music critic at *New York Magazine,* then a fledgling independent weekly. Music criticism turned out not to be my thing, and I found a niche instead doing real estate features. These stories had to be rich enough in human drama to engage readers who thought they had no interest in real estate (including me). Some of the real estate moguls I met were often either too bombastic or too tight-lipped to make for engaging interviews. And their focus could be narrow. Then, in the early 1970s, a press agent named Gerry Freeman urged me to meet Julien Studley, a client who had just finished up a deal that was very big and very secret.

I'd recently interviewed another real estate type, owner of a brace of office towers, whose reception room was dominated by a gilded, unabridged dictionary with unthumbed pages on an ornate stand and a large antique globe. Handsome old leather-bound books lined the shelves. All these items struck me as being nothing more than props. So it was refreshing to enter the smallish reception area of Julien J. Studley, Inc., then at 342 Madison Avenue, and find it dominated by a Ping-Pong table. Whatever else motivated this firm, it didn't seem to rule out having a little fun in the office.

Julien Studley, then in his late 40s, was a large-featured, bearded man whose manner was courtly yet aloof. His eyes were thoughtful and his large ears tilted slightly forward, which I later came to believe was the result of listening alertly to everyone who had something to say to him. His ears had simply adapted. Julien did have an interesting deal to talk about, as his press agent had claimed, but our conversation turned first to a pair of paintings on his desk, both recently acquired. One was a small, abstract collage done in 1934 by Le Corbusier, the iconic Swiss architect. This painting interested him, Studley explained, because it represented an unfamiliar phase of Le Corbusier's career.

The other painting was a nude by Suzanne Valadon, mother of Maurice Utrillo, the Parisian painter famed for his street scenes in Montmartre. Utrillo's paintings were usually signed "Utrillo V.," said Studley. Having been born out of wedlock, the "V" acknowledged his mother. She had been a teenage painter's model at the time of his birth.

"Valadon wasn't a great painter," said Julien, "but she was good, and she has a place in art history. I thought it would be nice to have one of her paintings."

That reasoning conveyed to me an early sense of how Julien could chart a course off the mainstream and yet do it for perfectly good reasons. Although another realtor might have bought a streetscape signed "Utrillo V.," familiar to all, Julien bought an unfamiliar painting signed by "V.," the artist's mother.

Our interview—more a wide-ranging conversation—came at the end of the work day and rolled on easily. Around seven o'clock, the phone rang. The switchboard had long since closed, and Julien picked it up.

"Yes, this is he," said Julien, and then listened patiently to the caller's rather long monologue. Eventually, he broke in gently: "Sir, what language would you be most comfortable speaking?"

In the next instant, the English portion of the conversation ended and restarted in what sounded to me like a Slavic language.

"Were you speaking Polish?" I asked after the end of the conversation.

"Russian," Julien answered. I didn't know yet that he could have equally carried on in Polish or an array of other languages, or that his mother tongue was French.

Julien told me that his firm was planning a winter trip for work and play that January. "To the Carribean?" I asked.

"To Chichicastenango."

It wasn't until I checked in my Columbia Desk Encyclopedia that I learned that this destination was an Indian market city in the mountains of Guatemala.

The Ping-Pong table, Julien's choice of art, the conversation in Russian, and the trip to Chichicastenango were early indicators that Studley was a real estate brokerage marching to the beat of a different drummer. Plainly, that drummer was Julien. It would take longer for me to understand that his rhythms and style, even when they departed from the MBA textbook, did not seem to hinder business. Julien J. Studley, Inc. (now simply Studley) always made money except in 1971, and in certain later years, scads of it.

In the lobby as I departed, I mentioned my love of Ping-Pong as a kid. "Shall we play a game?" asked Julien. I won the first few points. And then, quietly, diligently, and exceedingly politely, he trounced me.

Gerry Freeman had not exaggerated. Studley's deal, involving the midtown assemblage of the block on which Citicorp Center was soon to rise, was large, twisty, and newsworthy. My story on how the deal was done in *New York Magazine* was probably the best real estate story I ever wrote. It all but wrote itself.

Twenty-five years passed before I next heard from or saw Julien Studley. Then, late in 1999, I again visited him at his office, now a block-long, full floor at 300 Park Avenue, opposite the Waldorf-Astoria Hotel. What had been a small firm was now much expanded, with 15 offices nationwide, Studley was now, quite possibly, the largest commercial brokerage of its kind: never gone public, never franchised, and focused on leasing office space to the exclusion of retail renting or property management. The firm's growth had occurred without the aid of acquisitions or borrowing.

On the long wall of a corridor leading to the lobby, a collage of several hundred snapshots, although untitled, was clearly a travelogue of the firm's many winter trips. They included brokers wrestling alligators, running from bulls, horsing around in kilts, and caked in Dead Sea black mud. And not a single shot of anyone playing golf. In the lobby, a handsome Tang dynasty figure of a man was on display. Disappointingly, the Ping-Pong table was gone, although it later turned up in the foyer of Julien's apartment on East 60th Street, or rather apartments. In a residential replay of the Citicorp assemblage, Julien had put together four units on the 32nd and 33rd floors of his building, creating a rambling home with seven bathrooms—a rare number for an apartment.

Julien's beard was grayer, and the cut of his suit was now Saville Row, but otherwise he had changed little. The Corbusier collage hung directly behind his desk. Another Corbusier was at the door. Julien's ears still canted forward to catch every word spoken to him. As he showed me around the offices, I noticed a wall near the canteen and copy room being painstakingly sanded down by several workmen. If this was a simple repainting job, their pains seemed excessive.

"Actually," said Julien, "these fellows work for Sol LeWitt, the conceptual artist. I commissioned him to do an art project on this wall." The finished work would turn out to be a miniature version, in similar brilliant jags of primary colors, of LeWitt's lobby murals executed for Christie's auction room lobby at Rockefeller Center.

LeWitt asked $60,000 for that mural, Julien told me. Then the negotiating began. Julien had accepted that LeWitt's two versions of the work had been faxed over in standard 8″×11″ format. But he found it harder to accept that LeWitt would not personally execute the work. The workmen I had seen sanding down the wall would do that. "Do I want to pay $60,000 to a guy who isn't even painting it?" Julien had said to Matthew Bialecki, then his architect and art advisor.

"Let's set up a meeting," said Bialecki. When LeWitt arrived at Julien's office, Bialecki was struck by the feeling that "this guy could have been Julien's brother. They were both balding and a little paunchy. They exchanged some pleasantries and I saw that they both have this kind of retiring thing. Yet here were two titans."

Julien opened the negotiation, "by playing the rube," says Bialecki. He said to LeWitt, "My hat's off to you. But I'm struggling. It's $60,000, and you're not even painting it yourself?"

"It's not really that difficult to understand for somebody in your business," said LeWitt. "You conceptualize a deal. But there are plenty of people who could execute it better than yourself. Wouldn't you agree?"

Julien did. But one other item remained to be negotiated. Julien explained that his firm's lease was about to expire. "If we move elsewhere, we'd have to leave your work behind," he said. For a work that might be temporary, $60,000 was too high a price.

"No problem," said LeWitt. So a deal was crafted: Julien would pay $40,000 up front for the work on the wall. For $20,000 more, he would get the copyright and a certificate of authenticity. This would allow the firm to reproduce the work if and when it moved to new space. Julien and LeWitt shook hands.

The only souvenir of the Citicorp deal that I saw in the office was also on the wall: A painting by the late Keith Haring showing a yellow flying saucer aiming a red-glowing energy beam at the slant-sided crown of Citicorp Tower. "I thought that it might be fun for Citicorp to borrow the painting," said Julien. "But they rejected it. They had no sense of humor about this subject." And this was before 9/11.

Our meeting that day was a preliminary discussion about this book. Julien was then 73, and so strong was his imprint on Studley that it seemed impossible to think of the firm without him at the helm. But at the beginning of 2003, the baton passed to Mitch Steir, the firm's magnum dealmaker in the midtown Manhattan office. Steir became chairman and CEO. The firm is now simply called Studley. Julien remained as its founding chairman until the spring of 2004, which marked the 50th anniversary of the start of the firm in Julien's apartment.

This is the story of how, in those first 49 years, an immigrant kid, unsure of himself and unschooled in business, developed and led a company whose culture struck a balance between fun, camaraderie, and making money. And how the deals, at their most inspired, were raised to an urban art form. However, Julien does not point to the deals—and certainly not to the big money made—as his peak achievement. His biggest pride is in having developed a cadre of brokers who, in many cases, became hugely successful despite starting out with unpromising résumés. Last year's second-highest earner in the firm, for example, had only shown on her résumé that she had been a dental technician. A chapter in this book is devoted to her deals of deals. "The thing about Julien," says the architect Matt Bialecki, "is that, just when your patting yourself on the back for having done something terrific, he'll gently challenge you to take yourself to the next level."

Finally, this book is about how Julien took himself to the next level after his long run at business building. That was when he shifted over from real estate broker to full-time people broker.

Peter Hellman
New York, 2004

Deals

The art of the deal is more important than the technical notion of the deal.

—Julien Studley

It's all but automatic for us to assume that landmark urban real estate projects are hatched in the minds of architects, city planners, developers, and ambitious mayors. Yet, as this account of a firm called Studley, founded by Julien J. Studley shows, certain urban landmarks are first a gleam in the mind of a commercial real estate broker. But a gleam is not enough. Without the broker's ability to do the deal that clears the way, the great project may never be built.

When the project is completed, it will be the architects, city planners, developers, and mayors who will take their bows and get the press. The broker, who started it all, most likely will go unnoticed—athough her or his anonymity may be handsomely compensated.

Big Deal in Manhattan

Consider a pair of Studley brokers who, one Saturday morning in September 1968, emerged from a cab at the southeast corner of East 54th Street and Lexington Avenue in midtown Manhattan. On that corner was 60-year-old St. Peter's Lutheran Church. In its prime, when the area was still residential, St. Peter's boasted a congregation over a thousand strong. That number had dwindled to 300. Amid a sea of lively commerce, the old stone church looked a bit adrift.

The two brokers stood long in front of St. Peter's. Then, pausing frequently to take notes, they traversed all four sides of the block between 53rd and 54th Streets, and Lexington and Third Avenues. Here was a dense and diverse urban world in a rectangle. You could dine at leisure in a classic French restaurant, or grab a deli sandwich or a slice of pizza. You could linger over a beer at either of two old-fashioned bars on the block, have a prescription filled, buy a chic dress, or pick up your hometown newspaper at a news agent whose stock ranged from the *Cleveland Plain Dealer* to *Die Zeit.* One of the largest buildings on the block was the dowdy Medical Chambers building on 54th street. Although most residential uses had been pushed off the block long since, a handful of old-timers still lived in townhouses along 53rd and 54th Streets.

Not a soul on the block knew it, but a countdown had started that morning with the arrival of the two brokers. In five years' time, every building but one—31 in all—would be demolished. In their place would rise Citicorp Center, the silvery, 70-story office tower whose slant-sided apex would take its place with the Empire State and Chrysler buildings and—until that perfect blue morning on which they were cut down—the World Trade Center's twin towers as the most assertive markers of the Manhattan skyline. St. Peter's Church, alone among the buildings fated to be demolished, would be reborn as a cornerstone of the Citicorp complex, standing once again on its familiar corner. This time around, with its starkly modern design, the church would give a feeling of being anchored rather than adrift.

Thousands of workers would spend two years erecting Citicorp Center (later renamed Citigroup Center, a name that has not displaced the original name any more than Avenue of the Americas has replaced Sixth Avenue). Yet it took only those two Studley brokers to assemble the block—an undertaking every bit as intricate and as time-consuming as creating the mighty skyscraper. And while construction was a highly visible process, the assemblage had to be conducted in strictest secrecy in order not to be stymied by "holdouts." Alert eyes on the block would have seen no change, but alert minds must have formed their suspicions as properties and leases steadily were bought up. But nobody, apparently, guessed the identity of the real purchaser, even though the rear of Citibank's headquarters (it was then called First National City Bank), stood directly across Lexington Avenue from St. Peter's Church. (The bank fronted on Park Ave.)

At the time of the assemblage, the bank had more than 40,000 employees worldwide. Fewer than a dozen were privy to the secret undertaking. Even fewer knew the identity of Donald Schnabel and Charles MacArthur, the two Studley brokers assigned to carry it out. Except among hardcore real estate types, the name of their firm also would have drawn a blank.

Site of Sites

Shift the scene now to a very different sort of urban parcel, a half block across from the Mall in Washington, D.C. It abuts the Canadian Embassy at Pennsylvania Avenue and Sixth Street NW. Since 1961, the site had belonged to the District of Columbia's Department of Employment Services (DES), housed in a bland and scruffy five-story building. Frankly, given its placement directly across from the National Gallery of Art and one block from the National Archives, this site deserved a more fitting neighbor than a shoddily housed employment and retraining agency. Besides, the address was inconvenient for the agency's clientele, most of whom commuted from poor sections of the city. People who could afford to live near the Mall were not likely to enlist in the job training programs offered by the DES.

The potential of the property was there for creative minds to see. No other comparable location between the Capitol and the White House was available for new development. But change would not come easily, even if the DES building could be razed and its functions transferred elsewhere. Normally, the first step toward a new use of the site would be for the city to issue a request for proposals (RFP) to develop the site.

Any RFP was sure to be a long and creaky affair, the more so for such a prized site, and the D.C. government had a reputation for grinding its bureaucratic gears at low speed. Yet, starting in the spring of 2000, a Studley broker named Lois Zambo was able to shift the city into high gear on behalf of a determined and cash-heavy client, the Freedom Forum. A nonprofit offshoot of the Gannett newspaper chain, the Freedom Forum had spawned the Newseum, a museum dedicated to the media and the First Amendment, at that time hidden away amid a warren of faceless office towers in Rosslyn, Virginia, just across the Potomac River from Washington.

After four start-up years in Rosslyn, and with its lease soon to expire, Freedom Forum was eager to move this increasingly popular attraction to a more central site in Washington on the tourist trail. Ambitious as they were, Freedom Forum executives did not dream of relocating to the Mall until Zambo brought them to see the DES building and suggested that it be replaced by the Newseum.

Securing the site for the Newseum, Zambo warned, would be a torturous process. First, the city would have to be induced to relocate the DES. Then, once an RFP was issued, Freedom Forum would have to fight it out with other potential developers of the site. The winning proposal would require approval of the mayor, city council, local and federal agencies, and community activists. The process could take years, and even then it could fail.

"We don't want to go through an RFP," Charles Overby, president of the Freedom Forum, told Zambo. "But we do want the site." And Overby wanted swift action, so that the deal could be closed by the time the Newseum's current lease expired.

To a less resourceful and determined broker, Overby's wish might have seemed like a pipe dream. But Zambo proposed a battle plan whose objective was to swiftly secure the site for the Newseum by bypassing the requirement for an RFP. Her strategy called for overpaying by double the site's assessed value of $50 million: a cool $100 million cash. Twenty-five million dollars of that sum would be reserved for new, much needed low-income housing elsewhere in the city. But the offer was good only if the city agreed to sign the deal with unprecedented speed.

Acting rather than reacting, Zambo determined who had to be won over—and how—in the march toward her client's objective. Where she could not jawbone, she launched preemptive strikes to neutralize opposition. In the end, there was none. In October 2000, six months after Newseum executives first saw the site, the D.C. city council voted to sell it to the Freedom Forum without ever calling for an RFP.

Goodbye DES, hello Newseum.

Big Bucks, Less Respect

Commercial real estate brokerage is thought to lack glamour. Ambitious young people interested in business may aspire to be lawyers, investment bankers, accountants, consultants, or entrepreneurs. Being a space broker is rarely their ambition—although they might reconsider if they knew the megabucks that a good year can bring in. Of around 250 brokers at Studley in 2000 (admittedly a great year), 27 made more than $1 million. Even in the lean year of 2002, 10 brokers at the firm surpassed that mark. Rather than exercising stock options to make a bundle, these brokers earned their seven figures the old-fashioned way. Finding a fit between tenants and landlords, they closed the deals.

The common perception is that brokerage is a calling strictly for plodders who spend their days trudging between office buildings in the hope of finding tenants willing to move. Every broker has done that. Yet, as the Citicorp and Newseum deals show, mere trudging, no matter how determined, won't get you to the goal. Brokers need to grasp a vision and let nothing shake them loose from it if they are to be at the genesis of landmark projects. Had not Studley brokers pointed their clients to a path not yet seen, it is likely that neither the Citicorp headquarters nor the Newseum would be at their current locations.

It wasn't enough for the brokers to point the way. They also had to clear the way—a process that was as secretive in the case of the Citicorp assemblage as it was public in gaining the Newseum site. Money alone was not enough to get either deal done, any more than weapons alone suffice to win a war.

These two giant deals did not spring out of a neutral corporate environment. They were nourished by the offbeat but empowering culture of Studley and its founder. The new management team led by Mitch Steir is composed entirely of Studley brokers who are the kind of imaginative dealmakers that have always defined this firm. Their accession came in the aftermath of 9/11 and the popping of the dot-com balloon. It was an uncertain time in the world of commercial real estate. That's a good time for inventive and determined brokers.

Studley had a few dozen employees and two branch offices when the Citicorp assemblage was completed in 1974. As Freedom Forum took title to the Newseum site in 2000, the firm had grown to over 400 employees in 15 offices nationwide. Revenues in that 26-year period rose from $11 million to $185 million. Despite the ups and downs of the real estate cycle, the firm even eked out a profit in 2001, a year when many real estate brokerages bled. In the weak market of 2003, its first year under Mitch Steir's leadership, the firm continued its profitable ways.

Studley has come a long way from its modest birth in Julien's walk-up apartment in 1954. Yet, despite steady growth nationally, the firm never made "boosting the numbers" its top priority. Although other brokerages expanded through acquisitions, took on debt, went public, or got themselves bought (as market leader Cushman & Wakefield did by the Rockefeller Group, which was itself bought by Mitsubishi), Studley resisted all such moves. It stayed focused on creative deal making and kept its growth entirely internal, and self-financed even as it expanded nationally.

In this era when much corporate rot and greed have been detected, most scandalously at Enron, WorldCom, Tyco, and Parmalat, Studley's conservative bent, easy to scorn in go-go years, now gets respect. With the firm's stock held solely by employee retirement plans and by individual employees, shares awarded via stock options cannot be dumped on the public. They can only be sold back to the firm. When employees do sell back stock, they have always profited.

Studley's book value has increased steadily over the years, reflecting the firm's real growth. The stock has risen accordingly and has avoided the price plunges endemic to the stock market. Under Julien, the firm remained debt free. "If I'd gone to business school," says Julien with a laugh, "by now I'd either have a much larger company or I'd be bankrupt!"

Deal Hunting

Apart from a relatively compact headquarters cadre and salaried administrative workers in the branch offices, almost everyone at Studley is a commission broker, constantly seeking the scent of the next deal. "I come, I see, I smell," is how a mid-level broker describes his daily prowls through

Manhattan office towers. "If the elevator door opens on a floor that's vacant or under construction, then I investigate. Maybe the space is in play. Maybe a tenant needs my services." Most, but not all, brokers, leave the walking to younger brokers if they become successful. Richard Marek, 35 years at Studley before starting his own firm in 2003, specialized in big space deals for major law firms and investment banks, notably Lazard Frères. Yet the slender, perpetually tanned Marek was rarely at his desk, preferring to prowl the office turf of Manhattan.

Cold calling to lists of companies, like telemarketing, is rarely fruitful. But if handled artfully, it can pay off big. John Conerty, a broker in Studley's Chicago office, showed the right technique, a few years after joining Studley in 1993, in a cold call to the real estate director of Sears, Roebuck and Company. "I asked him if we could set up a meeting to discuss ideas about how to reduce the cost of his office space," says Conerty, "and he just kind of laughed."

Sears' real estate director explained to Conerty that under him was a staff of over 100 people. "They are all focused on reducing costs," he said. "What could you possibly do that they aren't already doing?"

"What percentage of your staff is dedicated to handling office space?" asked Conerty.

The director hesitated before admitting that he wasn't able to answer that question. Neither was he able to tell Conerty how many square feet of office space Sears was using.

"Would it be safe to assume that you have around 2 million square feet of office space nationwide?" asked Conerty.

"About that."

"And would you estimate that your you're paying an average of $20 per square foot for space?"

"That's a safe assumption."

"So that equates to spending $40 million annually on office space. What if I could save you $10 million of that? How would your department look if you could show them that?"

Conerty remembers a long pause. "Then he asked me how soon we could set up a meeting. His problem was that all the 100 or more people in the department were retail experts. He could have trained them to deal with office space, but it made more sense to outsource to us since we were already experienced. Once we got the assignment, we analyzed all of Sears leases and highlighted those that were higher than the prevailing market. We either restructured those leases or relocated offices to less expensive properties. On one project alone, we saved them $10 million. In all, it grew to about $30 million over seven years—more than we had promised them."

And all from a cold call. For anyone contacted by Conerty who happens to be a football fan, however, it needn't be totally cold. Conerty was a star running back of a championship team at the University if Miami in Ohio and is always ready to talk football.

Nothing even the best brokers did before coming to the firm gives them a leg up on what they must do here: Fashion the deal, fight for it, and seal it. Unlike a salesperson hawking televisions, a broker doesn't offer a defined product ready to be unboxed. The client may be clueless as to what product will best serve his or her needs until the broker sketches out the contours of a new idea. In the mid-1990s, for example, Don Schnabel broached a startling concept to the management of Nasdaq, the over-the-counter securities exchange. Unlike the New York Stock Exchange, Nasdaq was a faceless entity that had made no serious effort to beckon the public. Why not take itself out of the shadows, Schnabel thought, by creating a high profile corporate center and an enormous electronic sign on the west façade of 4 Times Square, an eco-friendly office tower being constructed by Douglas Durst at earth's highest-profile urban crossroads?

The Nasdaq real estate officer that Schnabel had long dealt with was cold to the idea. The third time he called her, "she went kind of bonkers on me." Schnabel asked for permission to try out his idea on somebody in Nasdaq's marketing department. "You can do that," she said, "but you have to tell him that I disagree."

After viewing a multi-media presentation of 4 Times Square, the marketing man was convinced. "He asked me to give him the ball and he would run with it," says Schnabel. "Other people at Nasdaq had to be gotten on the team. Three weeks later, he called me to asked if I would hold the space for him."

Schnabel was disconcerted. A shopper might ask for a dress to be held for future purchase. But ask a landlord to put a hold on a mighty space at 4 Times Square? "I knew and trusted Doug Durst," says Schnabel. "So I told him I was in an awkward position. I asked him to negotiate with me as if he had to compete with three alternate locations that my tenant could go to. Naturally, Doug wanted to know who the tenant was. I promised to tell him at the end of the conversation. But only after he assured me that, honest Injun, this was his best deal. We each kept our promise."

Nasdaq's seven-story MarketSite at 4 Times Square is dominated by the always-in-motion, wraparound sign flashing market quotes and news. Built at a cost of $37 million, it is the largest LED sign in the world. It is a frequent flasher on television news shows and has its annual mega-moment on the countdown to New Year's Eve when the ball drops. If not for Schnabel's concept and determination to see it up in lights, the sign on the Broadway corner of 4 Times Square might be featuring vast images of torsos swathed in Calvin Klein underwear.

Not that every deal is exciting. Day in and day out, humdrum transactions—and plenty of plodding—get done at Studley, as they must. But the firm also cultivated in its ranks free and fluid thought, which when the right hour came, shaped itself into something exciting and profitable. Just as startling as Schnabel's idea for Nasdaq, for example, was Julien's proposal of a new home to Cravath, Swaine & Moore.

Since 1961, the prestigious law firm had been anchored at 1 Chase Manhattan Plaza in Lower Manhattan. A quarter century later, Cravath was ready to move to midtown. Conventional wisdom would have placed the firm in a superior building on Park or Fifth Avenues, or a few steps away. Julien had a quite different notion. The site that he had in mind was Worldwide Plaza, a 50-story tower under construction in the late 1980s at 825 Eighth Avenue at 50th Street. With its pyramidal, copper-clad roof—homage to Cass Gilbert's New

York Life Insurance Building on Madison Avenue at 26th Street—the building was first class in every way. But the neighborhood was not. Infested with porn theaters and rampantly seedy, it seemed like the last place such a law firm would want to go.

In fact, there were benefits to Cravath at Worldwide Plaza, including attractive rent, custom-designed offices, and a separate entrance and elevators for the law firm. But what would blue-chip clients think of this "scarlet chip" address? "I told David Schwartz, Cravath's lead real estate attorney, that his law firm was among the few that could make that move," says Studley. "They had the immense prestige to validate the neighborhood." In 1990, Cravath went where lesser entities had feared to tread, taking the top 12 floors of Worldwide Plaza.

Schwartz made a curious request during the negotiations in 1988. "One of Cravath's clients was Salomon Brothers, a Wall Street's giant," says Julien. "David Schwartz asked if one of Salomon's people could sit in on the negotiation of the deal. I said, 'Excuse me, but will you tell me exactly what you mean?' He explained that Salomon's real estate department could benefit from learning how to do deals like this one. They were not a party to the transaction. It was not typical to do this. But the client had asked me for a favor, and since it couldn't harm anything, I was happy to oblige."

That small courtesy led to an enormous new deal for Studley within months. The client was none other than Salomon, which had outgrown its current home at One New York Plaza in Lower Manhattan, where it had created the largest private trading floor in the world in 1970. In a hugely publicized chapter in city planning gone awry, Salomon thought it had already nailed down a high-profile new home at Columbus Circle. There, Mortimer Zuckerman's Boston Properties planned to build a gigantic new office building on the site of the drab, unloved Coliseum, which had been superceded by the larger Javits Center. The land alone was to cost $455.1 million when the deal was announced in 1986. Salomon arranged the financing and was slated to be the building's anchor tenant.

"They were going to pay this insane price, rationalizing that somehow it made sense" says Julien. "They were thinking like Wall Streeters." The stock market tumble in October 1987, on top of intense civic opposition to an overscaled building that would have cast a huge afternoon shadow on Central Park, killed the deal. Salomon, whose downtown lease was soon to expire, once more was seeking a new home. "This time," says Julien, "they decided they were going to hire a *real* real estate firm."

Salomon was initially looking for about 850,000 square feet of office space. At Studley's first meeting with the company, held in a conference room adjacent to Salomon's trading floor, executives asked how long it would take to survey the market for available space.

"You're a very large gorilla," said Don Schnabel. "There are not a lot of cages in the city that you can fit into. You'll have your answer quickly."

The cage that Salomon selected was the brand new 7 World Trade Center, across a plaza north of the Twin Towers. Larry Silverstein had completed the 47-floor, 2-million-square-foot tower just as Wall Street was on the verge of a downturn. The anchor tenant he had counted on, Drexel Burnham Lambert Inc., backed out in the wake of Michael Milken's junk bond debacle, leaving the building almost entirely vacant. Studley now had come to the rescue with its "gorilla" in tow. But the negotiations went neither smoothly nor quickly. For one thing, Salomon wanted an equity share in the building in return for becoming the anchor tenant. Despite Julien's personal best effort, Silverstein refused to give up even a smidgen of ownership. John Gutfreund, the strong-willed chairman of Salomon, who once had both hired and fired one Michael Bloomberg, thought he could succeed where Julien had failed. He invited Silverstein to his office for a lunch at which he was determined to come away with a piece of 7 World Trade Center. Don Schnabel arrived at Salomon's office just as the lunch ended. He saw by the look on Gutfreund's face that Silverstein had stood fast. There was to be no equity deal.

A major worry of Silverstein, according to Schnabel was Salomon's right to sublet during the course its lease. Typically, landlords may not unreasonably withhold approval to sublet if the tenant no longer needs all its space. Silverstein was obsessed, in particular, with the possibility that if Salomon downsized, it might sublet to some unglamorous city agency that would bring down the tone of his building. So what if it paid the rent on time? "Larry refused to say that he would not unreasonably withhold permission to sublease," says Schnabel. "He said, 'What if Salomon goes to court and gets a judgment that I unreasonably withheld the right to sublet? Some guy in a black robe who makes $100,000 per year [a pittance to a big real estate player] could take my building away from me!'"

Studley custom-crafted an arbitration procedure to deal with Silverstein's obsession. Three arbitrators were picked. They were paid $5,000 per year with annual increases simply to be on call at short notice. If a subtenant proposed by Salomon were rejected by Silverstein, Salomon had four days to notify one of the arbitrators. Within 48 hours, the proceeding had to start. Salomon had just two days to present its case. Silverstein then had two days to present his side. At the end of the next day, the arbitrator's decision would be announced. Compared to most arbitrations, the speed demanded here was supersonic. If the ruling was that Silverstein had unreasonably withheld permission to sublet, he could still refuse the subtenant. Then Salomon could bring a lawsuit. "We told Larry that if that happened, he would already have two strikes against him," says Schnabel. "First, he had withheld permission to sublet. Then the arbitrator had ruled he had been unreasonable. So he'd have nobody to blame but himself if the man in the black robe who 'only' made $100,000 ruled against him."

The lease negotiations, lasting up to 15 hours at a stretch, continued seven days a week for three months. They were held at the office of Silverstein's attorney, Carb, Luria, Glassner, Cook & Kufeld. That firm was small, while Salomon's law firm, Wachtell, Lipton, Rosen & Katz, was among the biggest. "The lead lawyer for Salomon kept inserting changes by hand," says Julien, "and because his firm had an all-night operation, while Silverstein's didn't, those changes would show up the next morning proofread and woven into the lease. That overnight capability gave Salomon a huge advantage. Normally, it's the landlord's lawyer who keeps control of the lease."

The grueling negotiations took a personal toll on all parties at the table. Salomon's lead lawyer often slept over week nights at the Waldorf Astoria after delivering his changes to the night crew at his office, according to Schnabel. One Sunday morning, the normally prompt lawyer appeared several hours late for the daily meeting. "He explained that his young daughter had grabbed him by the leg and wouldn't let go as he was leaving the house," says Schnabel. "My own wife told me, 'Don, you don't seem to live here any more.'"

Finally, all the exhausted parties drew a line in the sand: Negotiations would wrap up on Thanksgiving Eve, 1988. And so they did. The signed lease with addenda was just over 1000 pages long, single-spaced. It covered details from as small as the "chemical-coated rag" to use on lobby metal work, and design details of the two flags Salomon was permitted to run up the poles on the plaza. The lease called for rent of $44 million per year for 1.1 million square feet, or more than $100,000 per *day*. Over its 20-year duration, the lease was valued at $1 billion. Acting as a consultant to the tenant rather than its broker, Studley was paid just over $2 million.

Even though the lease seemed to be precise, there were glitches. One year after it was signed, for example, Julien got a call from a top Salomon executive. He wasn't happy. The firm had received an annual real estate tax bill calling for $500,000 more than was scheduled by the lease. Had Studley screwed up? Julien sent Schnabel to investigate. The discrepancy was the direct result of Julien's dictum that as buildings get older, they get roomier. In the case of 7 World Trade Center, Silverstein had apparently allowed the building's advertised size to creep up. As owner of the land beneath the building, the Port Authority billed Salomon for taxes (actually PILOT, or payment in lieu of taxes). By Salomon's calculation, it had leased slightly under half of the building. By the Port Authority's reckoning, the firm was leasing slightly over half. When Julien brought the discrepancy to Silverstein's attention, he reduced Salomon's bill by $500,000. "I told Larry," says Julien, "that his mother would be proud of him. He loved his mother very much and often had her to lunch."

Salomon seemed confident of its future at 7 World Trade Center. So confident that, one morning during the negotiations, a Salomon executive informed Schnabel, "The boys on the trading floor had a great day yesterday. We'll take another 200,000 square feet." Just like that. In 1991, the year after Salomon moved 3,000 employees into 7 World Trade Center, the firm was caught in an illegal bidding scheme for Treasury securities. John Gutfreund resigned as chairman. The once proudly independent Salomon, first subsumed into Smith Barney in 1997 and then into Citigroup in 1998, is now just a cog in a vast financial machine.

Back when the lease at 7 World Trade Center was being hammered out, Salomon insisted on the right to install an emergency generating system with fuel tanks that could keep its trading floor running for days rather than hours in a blackout. Salomon's main fuel tanks were installed along with those of another tenant in the building, the mayor's Office of Emergency Management. Additional "day tanks" were installed on the specially reinforced fifth floor above the Consolidated Edison substation. The igniting of those tanks as the Twin Towers collapsed on the morning of September 11, 2001, sending flaming debris cascading down on surrounding buildings, may have also caused the conflagration at 7 World Trade Center. The building collapsed at 5:20 P.M. that afternoon, something no steel frame skyscraper of its type had ever done before that morning. And to think that Larry Silverstein's worst scenario was an undesirable subtenant!

Tweaking the Lease

Studley routinely seeks new space for its clients, as it did for Cravath and Salomon. Sometimes, it handles the situation differently, as when a team of brokers decided that the most creative way to deal with a big client's perceived need to move was to find ways to allow it to stay put. Time Inc. was such a client. In the mid-1990s, the publisher's stable of magazines was all but spilling out of its million square feet of space at the Time & Life building at 1271 Avenue of the Americas. Where to expand?

Next door, proposed Studley. A legal way was found for Time Inc. to sunder the west wall of its own premises and connect to the office building directly to its west on 50th Street. That building had been built for the American Management Association, which had long since departed. Now called the Sports Illustrated Building, it is connected to the "mother ship" through a handsome new multilevel glass-faced passageway. That solution proved to be as tricky for the architects as for Studley: due to an unforeseen pressure gradient between the two buildings on a windy day, the glass blew out.

Most deals don't approach the scale or inventiveness of those involving Citicorp, Newseum, Nasdaq, Cravath, Salomon, or Time Inc. But even the so-called average deal, in which a broker finds space for a client and negotiates a lease, is rarely simple. How much of the advertised space is usable? What givebacks will the landlord offer to "build out" the space to suit the tenant? What about subleasing and lease renewals? Options to expand or contract? Building management issues? Escalation clauses? Tax implications? Security? Telecom connections? Signage? How about "tech traps" that don't become evident until it's too late? Are there, for example, tinted windows that might contain metals that can compromise cell phone transmission?

Even a tenant's sense of whimsy can figure into a lease. During the era when the horizon seemed limitless for Internet start-ups, for example, a new company was looking for 20,000 square feet of space in San Francisco. But when a Studley broker located seemingly ideal space, the very young dot-commers rejected it. What they really wanted was a two-level space with vertical access via a firepole. They were only satisfied when the broker came up with a duplex pair of 10,000-square-foot floors. A firepole was duly installed between them. It may have been used for a quick exit when the bubble burst.

There was no whimsy in the predicament of a Milwaukee law firm whose lease in the city's largest office building was several years away from expiration. The partners preferred to renew the lease, but the landlord played tough. Confident that no other building in the city had enough available space to accommodate the law firm, this owner was unwilling to make a deal on any terms but his own.

Los Angeles-based Howard Sadowsky, the veteran broker representing the tenant, put the owner on notice that his client would move to a brand new building if meaningful concessions were not forthcoming. The owner was not impressed by that threat. He pointed out that the Milwaukee pipeline held no new buildings.

"My client will build its own new quarters," responded Sadowsky. The owner didn't believe that the law firm would "put on a hard hat" and play the role of developer. Then the game got serious.

The law firm, at Sadowsky's suggestion, bought an option on a commercial plot site outside the central city. It hired an architect to draw up preliminary plans for a new office building. Sadowsky made sure these steps came to the notice of the owner, who realized he no longer could take it for granted that he had a captive tenant. The prospect loomed of entire empty floors in his building. Filling them would not be easy. Fruitful negotiations with the law firm now became the order of the day. A lease renewal deal was signed, including concessions previously rejected by the owner. "The cost to the tenant of purchasing an option on a site and hiring an architect was less than $100,000," says Sadowsky. "The savings over the term of the lease were far greater than that."

Just as one owner may hang tough, another may lean over backwards in negotiating with a potential tenant. Understanding distinctions among owners enabled Joe Learner, a broker in Studley's Chicago office, to negotiate a below-market rent for a tenant in a tight market that was otherwise highly favorable to owners. The building was first-class. Learner even won the right for his tenant to put its logo in the lobby at no extra cost. Why was the owner such a softie? Because it was a REIT (real estate investment trust), explains Learner. Unlike a private owner, the REIT must answer to its shareholders. This particular REIT was anxious to show, before the end of its fiscal year, that the office space in question was producing income and that the rent was secure for years to come. Making a deal on the tenant's terms, in this instance, was better than no deal at all so long as it was signed before the REIT's fiscal year ran out. Private landlords can be as stubborn as they please.

On occasion, Studley's defense of the tenant means proposing the equivalent of transgender surgery: converting the tenant into an owner. This operation could make sense, according to Arthur Greenberg of the Washington office, "when the tenant has a lower cost of capital than the owner of its building does." And especially when the building has been over-leveraged with debt which could result in eventual default—a predicament which can used as a lever for the tenant. Greenberg determined in 1997, for example, that the owner of Marriot International's headquarters building in Bethesda, Maryland, was over-leveraged and headed for default on its $190 million mortgage note. Marriot International's lease was to expire just as the mortgage matured. If the tenant moved out, that would be catastrophic for owner and lender.

Greenberg wanted a restructured lease for his client. At first, the lender and owner refused. One week before Marriot committed to new build-to-suit quarters, the lender and owner "sharpened their pencils" and agreed to a buyback of the existing mortgage note at a discount. Marriot then signed a new 23 year bondable lease, meaning that it would pay "come hell or high water." With that lease in place, the owner was able to place a new, less onerous loan on the 775,000 square feet building.

"Any kid will find the transaction when a 50,000 square foot lease has just three years to run," says Greenberg, who was an accountant before he was a broker. "One of our strengths at Studley is in seeing the deal that is not apparent. The deal we did for Marriot had not even been on their radar screen."

Neither had ownership of its headquarters been on the radar screen of the American Association of Retired People, a tenant in a building in Washington, D.C. since 1991. In the mid-1990s Studley proposed to the AARP that would be better off as an owner, and not only because of its ability to borrow at a low rate. Research of public documents showed potential financial problems among five different owners of the AARP's 559,000 square foot building. In 2000, the AARP bought its building for $204 million and now pays less for its headquarters as owner than it had as tenant.

A similar proposal was made to the Federal Reseve Board, which was renting an annex building in Washington. "The Fed's cost of funds was basically the same as that of the U.S. Treasury," says Greenberg. The only problem with purchasing the annex, the tenant pointed out, was that the FRB was forbidden by law from owning any building other than its headquarters. "We felt that it was wrong to let a stupid little law affect a good business deal," says Greenberg. The law was changed and the $67 million sale of the annex was completed in 2001.

Fighting for the Tenant

Studley's priorities and particular culture have been shaped by the controlling personality of the firm's founder. Although many real estate brokerages act as agent for the owner of a particular building, Studley declares itself to be on the side of the tenant. Here and there, the firm will cross sides if a particular opportunity arises, but on the whole, it has kept the faith with tenant interests.

There's a paradox here, since it's usually the landlord who pays the commission to the broker upon signing a deal. As the line goes in the Bob Dylan song, "You're gonna have to serve somebody." Robert W. Semenow's primer for brokers called *Questions and Answers About Real Estate,* ninth edition (Prentice-Hall Inc., Englewood Cliffs, N.J., 1978) states: "The interests of three persons are involved in a real estate transaction: the owner, the broker, and the purchaser, *with whom the broker negotiates in the interest of the owner* (italics mine).

How then can Studley or any other broker claim to serve the tenant if legally obligated to the owner, who also signs the commission check? Studley's answer is a contract with the tenant giving the firm the right to represent it in a lease negotiation. That allegiance will be made clear to the owner. The law and common practice recognize that a broker may be hired by the tenant and paid by the landlord. The argument is also made that, in any case, the owner pays the commission using the tenant's rent money. Track it back, and the tenant becomes the true payer.

Tenant orientation, set by Julien early on, is one of the firm's bases for success. Consider the situation in San Francisco. For the year beginning in the fourth quarter of 2000, rents in San Francisco sank from $71.57 to $32.81 per square foot. Clear-eyed brokers who sensed that market vector could have saved clients lots of money—more, probably, than brokers who represent owners and have no such incentive.

A broker not under an owner's thumb also has the freedom to scout for buildings in which a primary tenant may be willing to sublease space, even though it hesitates to put it on the market. This unlisted availability is called "shadow space." In 2003, Mitch Steir sensed that shadow space might be available at the Bertelsmann-owned office tower at 1540 Times Square. It was, and Steir quietly arranged to lease floors 18 through 23 to Pillsbury Winthrop LLP, a law firm which had long been in Lower Manhattan. Since the tenant giving up the space was a unit of Bertelsmann, Steir was able to negotiate a direct lease with the owner of the building for his client, including extension rights.

Strange Bedfellows

Even by the relaxed standards of brokerage, the criteria used by Studley to hire fledgling brokers can only be described as offbeat. No formal degree or even high school diploma is required to be a real estate salesperson or broker. It's enough to take a 45-hour course and to pass a state-administered test. Ambitious candidates sometimes pass the exam before they take the course. Julien himself, a man of broad culture and an educational activist, never did find the time to finish high school, having gone directly to work as a 16-year-old immigrant. His firm has numbered among its brokers a former hearse driver, a jewelry designer, a plasma physicist, an art historian, a modern dancer, a finance commissioner of New York City, several former hippies, a tennis pro, and even a few Harvard MBAs. In this eclectic group, the one who did least well as a broker was the former finance commissioner, while the art historian and modern dancer both soared.

Job interviews at Studley must be to tuned to talent, which can require adjusting the dial to unlikely frequencies. Years ago, for example, a senior broker interviewed a young applicant. He was fresh from a job working on a giant uranium mining machine in Utah. He was also an accomplished potter. His hair was long and blond.

"Tell me something interesting that you did in college," asked the broker.

"I built a doll house," answered Kurt Handschumacher.

Elsewhere, that response might have earned him a handshake and an escort to the elevator. But the broker leaned closer.

"Tell me more about the doll house," he said.

Handschumacher did better than that. He pulled out photos of the project, which he had brought with him. The doll house was filled with miniature period furniture which the young man had precisely crafted. Handschumacher got the job.

"I felt that anyone who could focus on that level of detail would bring the same care to brokerage," explains the interviewing broker.

Handschumacher rose to become the firm's first analyst to earn more than $1 million. Although his work might well be highly valued by an accounting or consulting firm, it's unlikely that his dollhouse would have been the springboard to a job.

Ted Rotante, a Studley broker beginning in 1979, left behind a career as a modern dancer. With his first wife, Nora (daughter of folksinger Woody Guthrie), Rotante had a dance company. "My knees were starting to act up, and I felt it was time to find something else," says Rotante. Julien conducted the interview. "He wasn't just dancing," says Julien. "He was also handling the bookings and finances of his dance company. Why couldn't he be effective outside of the arts?"

"Julien gave me a desk, a phone, and a small monthly draw," says Rotante. "I started by calling people working around the edges of the arts, a world I felt comfortable in." In 1985, Julien put Rotante in touch with a real estate investor he had met on an airplane. The investor and two partners had bought the old Haaren High School, vacant but fabulously ornate, on Tenth Avenue at 58th Street. Their plan was to convert it into video production studios. "The rent they could get wasn't enough to make it work," says Rotante. "Meanwhile, right across the street was John Jay College of Criminal Justice. Its lease was expiring. Putting John Jay in this great space was a no-brainer." The ex-dancer collected his firm's first commission exceeding $2 million.

In 1999, a fat time for brokers, Rotante took a cold call that didn't sound promising. An assistant to an executive in the cable television world was looking for 3,000 to 4,000 square feet of space. "When I asked who her boss was," says

Rotante, "she insisted that she really couldn't tell me. Still, I got a little jolt of electricity." The unnamed executive's space needs grew. The lease that she finally signed was for 100,000 square feet at Chelsea Market at Ninth Avenue and 16th Street. The client was Oxygen Media, and the unnamed executive was its chairman and CEO, Geraldine Laybourne. "The moral of the story," says Rotante, "is never throw a dollar bill on the floor." A few years later, Rotante aided Laybourne in downsizing Oxygen Media.

The success of Studley's offbeat hires, not limited to Handschumacher and Rotante, is more than dumb luck. It goes to the heart of Julien's leadership method, as pinpointed by Don Schnabel. "Many people think that Julien is very good at getting people to do what he wants them to do. But that's a fundamental mistake. Julien's managerial gift is to open up the space for people to meet their *own* possibilities."

Not every individual at Studley, however, may be psychologically ready to meet his or her own possibilities. Once, Julien was interviewing an assistant to a senior broker at a newly opened branch office in Dallas. The young man proudly told Julien that he was the first person from his family to go to college. He had even gone on to get an MBA. He was planning on soon becoming a junior broker, not merely an assistant. He smiled proudly. But instead of congratulating the interviewee, Julien stared at him in silence for a long moment.

"How long were you an assistant broker before coming here?" asked Julien.

"Several years."

"How much did you make last year?"

"$30,000."

Julien frowned. "I'm worried about your valuation of your own self in this job. You should be making more than $30,000 by now. Is it possible that, because you've accomplished what nobody else in your family has, you think you have gone far enough?"

"No, no," the young man answered.

"Then I would say to you that you need to have a passion to excel at some part of this business so that you can move up the ladder rapidly. If you're not making $250,000 in a year or two here, go find another business."

The young man gulped.

"If you do think that you've already accomplished enough here," continued Julien, "that's understandable but not acceptable."

Julien shook the young man's hand. "You knew you'd get a blunt view from me, right?"

"I guess I needed to hear that, Mr. Studley." It was time for the next interview.

Trips

Studley's offbeat culture shows up, sometimes strikingly, in its choice of destinations for the firm's annual winter trip, rewarding around 75 of the previous year's highest-earning brokers (commissions not less than $750,000 in 2000). Incentive trips are a bedrock of corporate sales culture, of course. Typical destinations might be Palm Springs, Hawaii, Paris, London, or a luxurious Caribbean beach resort. But

Studley's 30-odd winter trips have almost always bypassed the standard venues and left luxury far behind as the brokers packed their bags for places like Manaus, Cartagena, Huatulco, Yelapa, and (in the year I met Julien) Chichicastenango. They've been gored by bulls, cornered by scorpions, stranded in remote fishing villages, and made ghastly sick by microbes on the Nile or by heavy seas off Patagonia.

The most startling, even notorious, image from the winter trips was captured in 1990 by a photographer for *National Geographic* magazine on assignment in the Amazon Basin. It shows five men lashed to trees in the coffee-colored shallows of the Rio Negro, a tributary of the Amazon River. They are naked except for loincloths, and warpaint dabbed on their downturned faces. You might guess this scene is a throwback to an era of tribal wars in which the defeated warriors have been left by the victors to the untender mercies of a river teeming with piranhas, water snakes, and leeches.

In fact, this captive quintet is made up of Studley brokers on their first winter trip, here being initiated into the ranks of the firm's top earners. Back home, they've excelled at what war is usually about—winning turf for their clients against other combatants who would wrest it from them. Besides fending off competing brokers, they must also sometimes face off against landlords. As in war, uncertainties abound and the situation on the ground is often foggy or fluid. Without aggressive instincts, they'd never succeed. The story is told of a Studley broker, Mark Jaccom, who spent weeks fruitlessly trying to talk directly to the CEO of a Manhattan firm that was a potential client. In one of his numerous calls to the CEO's secretary, Jaccom was told that her boss would be unavailable all the following week because he was flying to Florida on Monday morning.

"Thank you," said Jaccom, and he hung up.

As the CEO took his first class seat on the flight to Florida, Jaccom was in the adjoining seat. By the end of the two-and-a-half-hour flight, the CEO had capitulated to superior reconnaissance and infiltration. Jaccom took over as the company's primary space broker. In 2003, as part of Studley's incoming leadership team, Jaccom became Vice Chairman of U.S. Operations.

Wired Up Early

Julien has long worked out of a modest-sized corner office on the third floor of 300 Park Avenue. Here at midtown's heart, his east-facing windows look out on the entrance to the Waldorf Astoria Hotel, with its perpetual bustle of taxis and tourists. From the north windows, the view is of Saint Bartholomew's Church with the pinnacled General Electric Building rising behind it. Beyond that, is the Seagram Building. Being close to the street, the view is surprisingly intimate. Fresh flowers always adorn Julien's office. His blond desk is clean-lined, as are the sofa and leather chairs. There is no bookcase, but the most striking absence might take a few moments to identify: This office is computerless.

Young brokers may have felt that, without a computer, their septuagenarian boss must be out of touch with technology. In fact, when laptop computers were first being marketed, Julien ordered two for the firm and for a while kept one on his desk. A charter subscriber to *Wired* magazine, Julien also saw to it that his firm was among the first brokerages to create a web site. And while one of Julien's key management themes is minimizing administrative staff, he did hire an information technology specialist in 1981, a time when the term was not well known.

"I remember Julien walking into my office over 20 years ago," says Tsun Tam, the man Julien hired. "He asked me if I'd ever heard of 'this thing called COMDEX.' Of course, I had. It's the annual show for business technology held in Las Vegas. It was only about a week until it was opening."

"You should be there," said Julien. "If you find anything interesting for us, give me a call. I'm staying at Binion's Horseshoe."

"It'll be expensive for me to fly on short notice, and besides, it's too late to book a hotel room," said Tsun Tam. "Las Vegas is packed for COMDEX."

"I'll get you a room," said Julien.

Tsun Tam did see something interesting: a new way to make multimedia presentations by IBM. "I thought it could be used at our summer outing and Julien agreed," he says. "We hired IBM to do it."

In the late 1980's, Julien queried Tsun Tam about the Internet, then in its infancy. "I told him that it was only a college slash government thing," says Tsun Tam, "and that only the geekiest guys used it. But he wasn't dissuaded. He wanted us to have the Internet."

Julien's self-judgment, seconded by his colleagues, is that he was never the firm's best broker. Not even close to the best.

To excel at brokerage requires a single-minded drive toward closing the deal that is the opposite of Julien's free-roving approach. His strengths have been to firmly shape a corporate culture that embraces offbeat but creative talent and to provide the platform from which deals can be done with the Studley stamp. Julien was also adept at getting the firm noticed in the press, especially when it was small. As times changed and the firm grew, he found routes to go forward and exerted the considerable force of his personality in keeping the peace among his often boisterous clan of brokers.

And they could be boisterous. I remember a winter trip luncheon at a restaurant on a quiet street in old Seville during the siesta hour. Quiet except for a Studley broker, pacing on the sidewalk, shouting into his cell phone to someone back in New York, "Listen, you tell him I put my balls on the line for him, so he better goddamn well do the right thing by me now..."

Early on, so-called "renaissance brokers" handled every aspect of a deal. Proverbially, they could do the numbers on the back of a napkin with a pencil in one hand and a deli sandwich in the other. But that model didn't work for national companies like Marsh & McClennan, Gateway, or Microsoft, all of which became Studley clients. Before settling on a location, these companies often demanded precise data on demographics, transportation, municipal incentives, and quality-of-life information markers. In the mid-1980s, Studley responded to these needs by creating a national accounts division. Brokers might now have to do troublesome little deals, not worth their time if taken individually, in the hope of more lucrative deals for the same client. For a firm that had long been known as a master of the one-off deal, this was almost a sea change.

In 1985, Studley hired Nicholas Borg to be the firm's chief operating officer. Borg, formerly a top executive with the New York City School Construction Authority, had no brokerage experience. Studley's brokers, out of whose commissions his handsome salary was paid, did not give Borg a warm welcome. Still, for the first time, Borg began to rationalize Studley's increasingly complex business practices.

From national accounts, it was a short step to the birth of teams of brokers, sharing commissions and using analysts, graphics and space designers, construction specialists, and even lowly cold callers for support. Here, indeed, was the sea change. Teams could swiftly create a sophisticated presentation that not even a renaissance broker could match for, say, a local law firm contemplating a move. The best of the behind-the-scenes team members are paid accordingly. When an analyst first earned over a million dollars in the 1990s, it was a potent sign that Studley's strength had shifted from the mythic renaissance brokers to interdisciplinary teams.

Still, this was the firm that had not gone the route of its competitors in the previous decades. The competition, as it grew, expanded services to include interior design, engineering, construction, and financial services—so-called "one-stop shopping." Studley had resisted that impulse despite the risk of losing clients who preferred the convenience of bundled services. The firm had also stayed clear of property management, even though "fixing toilet-stall doors," as Julien scornfully summarizes that bedrock business, can provide an income cushion in slack times for leasing. Weighing down the payroll with functionaries, according to the Studley view, slows the deal-making reflex. It's the workings of that reflex that these pages attempt to reveal.

Julien created an office of the president in 1997 in preparation for a transition to new leadership. By the spring of 2002, as he celebrated his seventy-fifth birthday in full vigor, no real transition at the top had occurred. But one was in the making. A group of 45 brokers, led by Mitch Steir, proposed to take control by buying out Julien and several other senior shareholders. Steir had built a team of brokers and analysts in the midtown Manhattan office that generated over $15 million in commissions in a single year. In a vote of confidence in the new management, each broker invested a minimum of $100,000 in the buyout—quite a contrast to companies in which executives unloaded shares as the market headed south. Or wished that they had. The transition, completed at the beginning of 2003, went smoothly.

Like the deals his firm is known for, Julien was a one-off leader. The boyish Mitch Steir has his own style, starting with his addiction to the fortunes of the Boston Red Sox (Julien's eclectic interests do not include sports). Still, inventive deal-making must remain the firm's core strength, as an incident in Argentina during the 2001 winter trip suggests.

After lunch at a restaurant on an island near Buenos Aires, the brokers heard a presentation by an executive with Zethus, a new and ambitious web-based brokerage services provider. Anxious to get Studley as a client, the Zethus salesman traveled from New York to make his 45-minute pitch on "automating many of the processes involved in leasing, buying and selling commercial property." But these several dozen brokers, sitting on a beflowered veranda, were cool to the claims touted for Zethus. In fact, they were downright stony-faced. Their instincts told them that, despite the executive's grandiose claims of a rosy future for his firm, it was sinking. They were correct. Zethus is gone.

After the executive departed in a waiting water taxi, Michael Colacino, now Studley's president, summed up both the brokers' judgment and his own firm's essence: "This guy missed the point," said Colacino. "He's trying to sell us a broker in a box. We're brokers outside the box."

2 Early Years

If you hear a bell, don't move until you know where the sound is coming from. Then be swift.

—Julien Studley

The instinct that detects danger may be the same as that which sniffs out opportunity. In either case, advantage comes only if action is taken. In boyhood, Julien's instincts were honed by mortal danger and upheaval. Later, they served him well in the real estate arena.

On May 13, 1940, the Studley family packed up and left their home in Brussels forever. Three days earlier, Hitler's army had invaded Belgium and neighboring Holland. Although the Belgian defenses to the east were expected to hold the Germans at least for a while, realistic minds, among them Max Studley's, concluded that this was no time to sit passively.

Lashed to the top of Studley's 1932 Buick, as the family departed, were two mattresses. They would be needed not only for sleep but possibly to protect against strafing by German fighter planes. In the Buick were Max and his wife,

Maria, both 40 years old, and their two sons: Julien, age 12, and George, age 9.*

Also a passenger was Michael Krainess, who was distantly related to Max. Now a de facto member of the Studley household, Krainess was called "Uncle Mischa" by the boys. The rest of the space in the car was filled with hastily packed suitcases.

The Studleys were at the leading edge of a rapidly swelling flow of refugees heading south toward France, which had not yet been invaded. Had they stayed behind, the Studleys soon would have been targeted by the German occupiers for deportation along with all other Belgian Jews. One-third of the 90,000 Jews in the country would be murdered at Auschwitz. Max Studley couldn't even suspect the unimaginable that spring. The only certainty was that it was time to act to protect the family.

Max, a strong-featured man with a Teddy Roosevelt–style mustache, had been born in Warsaw into a prosperous family with interests in beer. His grandfather, according to family lore, was a man of outsized appetite who could eat a dozen eggs at a sitting. Maria, darkly elegant, had been born in Kiev, Ukraine, into a wealthy family involved in railroad building. When Maria was still a girl, her family moved to Warsaw, installing itself in an elegant pair of apartments overlooking the local racetrack. Max and Maria met as students at the university in the "free city" of Danzig, now the

*The original family name was Stuckgold. After arriving in New York in 1944, Max picked the name Studley from the telephone directory. To avoid confusion, Studley is used throughout the text.

Polish city of Gdansk. Both of them earned extra money, by selling tire repair kits. Maria was the better salesperson. Her parents were not enthusiastic about the match. They would have preferred someone more religiously observant than Max.

Max went to Berlin and earned an engineering degree. He admired German culture, but Paris beckoned. That is where he and Maria planned to emigrate to after their marriage in Danzig in 1925. They sailed first to Antwerp, Belgium, and intended only to make a stopover in Brussels, where the couple had both relatives and friends. Somehow, they never left. Max found work as a controls engineer, representing German equipment manufacturers in Belgium.

Julien was born in 1927, George three years later. Although Max earned only a modest living, the boys grew up in a middle class atmosphere of warmth and culture. "The one time when we'd be permitted to stay up past our bedtime," remembers Julien, "was when there was a radio performance of great symphonic music—a Beethoven symphony, or something by Dvorák or César Franck, who was Belgian. My father would whistle a special tune to bring me and George home if we were playing outdoors or to call us together in a crowd. It was the theme from Dvorák's 'New World' symphony." Maria appreciated music, but her husband was smitten with it.

Before the war, the Studleys lived in an apartment with French balconies on the sixth floor of a building in a middle class neighborhood of Brussels. "Later, when my father was cut off by his German business partners as the Nazis became stronger, we moved to an old house," says Julien. "That was a step down, because a house was not then considered to be as fashionable as a good apartment. But it had advantages. We had a tenant, which helped to pay the rent. And my father had a garden in the back yard. He was far from being a farmer, but he loved to till the soil. He also loved dogs. We had a big, gray Bouvier and then a pointer. One summer, while my mom went off to visit her mother in Warsaw, the pointer died. She was the one who fed him and fussed over him and we thought that maybe he died from missing her."

Max was also "a whiz with art and furniture," according to Julien. He haunted the Brussels auction halls, buying for friends as well as his own family. "I remember four rooms that my father furnished," Julien says. "In the study were big, rounded upholstered chairs. The dining room table and chairs in Louis XIII style—a look that was more clunky than elegant. The salon was Louis XV and XVI. Upstairs, in my parents' bedroom, were a pair of large, gray and silver metal Art Deco beds."

Maria was a stylish woman, an adept housekeeper and a good mother. Julian remembers how, as a small boy, he numbered for his mother all the items that he would buy for her when he grew up. On top of the list was a very nice house. "I never thought of being wealthy," Julien explains. "I just wanted to be able to buy her things."

By the mid 1930s, the Reich's intensifying anti-Jewish policies meant that Max Studley was cut off from the German companies he had represented in Belgium. But he found a way to deal a small blow against the enemy. "One of my dad's clients showed him a set of blueprints for a gas monitoring system in a German submarine," Julien explains, "and he absconded with them. Then—this must have been about

1937—we drove to Paris and he delivered the blueprints to the French naval command. I remember waiting in our Buick parked outside the navy headquarters on the Place de la Concorde, waiting for my father to return." Julien has preserved a letter dated 9 December 1937 from the French naval ministry, scientific research division, thanking Max Studley for his "gracious donation." It promises to keep him "au courant" on further study of the plans.

On their first evening as refugees, the Studley family stopped at La Panne, a Belgian coastal town on the French border. In the following days, as the French historian Henri Michel described the gathering exodus, "A flood of humanity flowed in their millions . . . flung headlong on to the roads by the dreadful fear of what the morrow might have in store . . . cars, motor-cyclists, cyclists and horsedrawn carts all moving at a snail's pace because of the congested roads." Although Belgian citizens were permitted to cross the border, foreigners living in Belgium, including the Studleys, were refused entry into France without visas. Both Max and Maria had been born in 1900, when both Vilnius and Warsaw had belonged to the Czar. Legally, they were stateless—a situation that made them especially vulnerable.

Julien, wearing his Boy Scout uniform, volunteered to be a Red Cross aide in La Panne as refugees streamed through. "My brother was running errands and helping direct traffic in the town until our father could figure out what to do next," remembers George. Julien took his duties seriously, at one point even ready to report to the authorities two German-speaking men who had been pointed out to him as possible spies. Luckily, he first informed his mother. After interviewing the two "suspects" herself, Maria scolded Julien: "They are Jews who are running away from Hitler, just like us. Leave them alone."

The family tarried in La Panne, Julien remembers, because "my father thought that if our forces could be augmented by British troops, we might be able to hold the line. We all knew that when the Germans attacked Belgium in the First World War, King Albert said, 'They shall not pass.' And they didn't."

This time, the Germans would pass, and sooner rather than later. With Julien's Red Cross identification badge pasted on the windshield of the Buick, the Studley family crossed into France on May 18. They were part of the last Red Cross convoy to reach French soil before the border was closed. Snagging a ride with the family were two wealthy Berliners whom Uncle Mischa had met. Julien, still wearing his Boy Scout uniform, rode ahead of the car on his bicycle. "Father said that it would look like an official escort," says Julian. At the ferry terminal of Calais, the two Berliners boarded a boat for England. In gratitude for their border passage, they gave the Studleys the equivalent of $2,000 in gold coins—a resource which, in the coming months, would help to carry the family, which had limited cash of its own.

On their first night in France, the family stopped in the small seacoast town of Gravelines. It was Julien's thirteenth birthday. According to Jewish tradition, he was now a man. There was no formal bar mitzvah ceremony, but the family did acknowledge their first-born son's coming of age. Relatives from Poland—they would soon be murdered by the Nazis—

had sent Julien a set of phylacteries, small boxes containing scriptural passages which are donned at morning prayers by observant Jews. The Studleys were not observant, although Julien remembers being taken to synagogue twice on the High Holy days. On that night of his bar mitzvah, Julien heard the crackle of machine gun fire directed at German airplanes from an offshore barge. It was the first time he felt the proximity to this war that his family was trying to leave behind.

They traveled southward through France, away from the German fury. "My father was good at somehow getting us one last tank of gas when none seemed to be available," remembers George. "He also had a sense for how to find little country roads when the main arteries were choked with traffic."

Midway down the Atlantic coast, in Cognac country, the family went from farm to farm, looking for lodging. "The first few places didn't work out," remembers Julien, "but all the farmers insisted that before we left, my father needed a nip of cognac for the road. He got a little tipsy." The family finally found quarters at a farm where, among the usual animals, angora rabbits were raised and their fur plucked—a process that shocked Julien. On that farm, too, he first used an outhouse. "Over the seat there was a book anchored to a cord," he remembers, "so that you could read but not walk away with it." Julien loved the farm with its smells of cows and horses.

Six weeks after leaving home, the family reached the port city of Bayonne in southwestern France, almost at the Spanish border. The date was June 23, 1940. By then, France was a defeated nation, partitioned into a northern zone under German control and a Vichy state in the south led by Marshal Philippe Petain, hero of the First World War. In Bayonne, Max joined a crush of desperate visa seekers in front of the Spanish consulate, all hoping to be awarded the precious document that would admit them to neutral Spain. Max waited for 20 hours, sweating profusely in the intense southern heat. The supplicants at the gate endured more than the heat. French police cruelly tried to push them back from the consulate gate by hurling dead rats at them. Max's "superhuman effort," as Julien calls it, was fruitless.

A relative of Maria had better luck in Bayonne. He was Solomon Melup, who owned a factory that supplied gas masks to the Polish Army. Melup was himself an honorary officer in the supply corps. By chance, the Studleys recognized Melup amid a crowd of Polish soldiers who had made their way to France after Poland was crushed by the Nazis in the previous September. They were boarding a barge that would take them to Britain. "When the other soldiers discovered that Solomon was a Jew," says Julien, "they tried to throw him overboard." In fact, Melup had been appointed to be economic advisor to the Polish government-in-exile in London. According to Melup's daughter, Irene, he told the soldiers, "If I'm good enough to be in your government, I'm good enough to be aboard." That ended the fracas.

Blocked from entering Spain, the Studleys now drove eastward toward the French Mediterranean coast, stopping for a few days in the old section of Perpignan. Julien remembers going down a street so narrow that finally the Buick couldn't go any further, and then his father's tense and tortuous effort to back it out. The family headed on to

Montpellier, further along the sea coast. It was a pleasant place, and they settled into a decent hotel where they hoped to stay for a while. Then, one morning, the desk clerk whispered to them that "a nice German gentleman was checking license plate numbers of guests' cars during the night." The Buick was packed for immediate departure.

Despite the family's homelessness, its diminishing cash supply, and the German threat, Julien says that "when you're 13 years old, you don't feel those tensions. At that age, it's all an adventure for a boy."

The perigrinations that had begun in Brussels finally ended in Nice, where the Studleys and Uncle Mischa arrived at the end of June 1940. They found a modest apartment at 4 Petite Rue Emilia and settled into a seemingly normal routine. Julien and George were enrolled in school. George made friends with the son of the neighborhood tailor, a fascist who kept a bust of Mussolini on display in his shop. Although George was happy at school, Julien despised the authoritarian atmosphere in the classroom of his lycée. "You had to sit with your hands clasped in front of you," he says. Back in Brussels, he had loved his "enlightened" public school.

Max idled away his days playing bridge with other refugees at the old, elegant Hotel Ruhl, which George compares to the Hotel de Paris in Monte Carlo. Uncle Mischa frequented a cafe where he brokered black market currency. In the evenings, he accompanied Maria to the casino, where she did well because, according to George, "she was a very controlled player." Thanks to sponsoring relatives in New York, Uncle Mischa was issued a visa to enter America. For Jewish refugees feeling the Nazi shadow advancing on them in Vichy, a visa to the United States was precious. But Uncle Mischa did not use his. Julien says, "He stayed with us to be of help to the family."

In May 1941, almost a year after their arrival in Nice, Max and Maria registered with the French police as foreign nationals, as ordered by Vichy. Required to submit the name of a French citizen as a character reference, Max used the rabbit-raising farmer from whom the family had rented quarters in Cognac country. Daringly, the Studleys did not register as Jews, as required by Vichy anti-Jewish regulations. Julien remembers a domestic debate, carried on in the kitchen, that arose in many other Jewish families: to register or not to register by religion? Maria felt that it was prudent to obey the order. If it were flaunted and they were caught, the punishment would be grave. Max believed—correctly, as it turned out—that no good could come of registering as Jews. That information would soon enough be used to arrest tens of thousands of Jews in both the Occupied Zone and Vichy. Including Uncle Mischa.

As Vichy anti-Jewish measures increased, the Studleys knew they must find a way to flee France. "My father's idea was that we should try to rent a sailboat and cross to North Africa," says Julien. "He was always the dreamer." Maria took a more realistic tack. She "camped out" in the office of the Jewish community welfare office in Marseilles, a day's trip from Nice, until she had in hand visas for the family to Cuba, obtained with the help of the Melup family, which had made it to New York. Maria also wangled steamship tickets to Havana by way of North Africa.

The Studleys departed from Marseilles aboard the steamer *Gouverneur General Tiremont* in January 1942. Two days later, they docked in Oran, Algeria and were delivered to a transit camp near Casablanca, Morocco, until they could ship out for Cuba. Conditions in French internment camps at the time, the biggest of which was at Gurs, were cruel. But George remembers that the Moroccan camp "seemed like paradise, where we could eat eggs and fresh dates."

In that same month that the Studleys left France, the fate of millions of European Jews was being sealed at a secret conference convened by Reinhard Heydrich, head of the SS, in a lakeside villa at Wannsee, Germany. There, Adolf Hitler's decision to kill all European Jews was put into motion. One victim, from among the 76,000 Jews to be deported from France would be Michael Krainess. By the time he was ready to use his visa to escape to America, it was too late.

"Uncle Mischa was a Soviet citizen who worked as treasurer of the Soviet embassy in Berlin in the early 1930s," says George. "He had lots of German friends. We always thought some of those people might have helped him." According to documents located by Serge Klarsfeld, the French historian of the Holocaust, Krainess was arrested in Nice in the late winter of 1944 and was among 250 Jews transferred to Drancy, the transit camp just north of Paris. On March 7, 1944, he was deported to Auschwitz, from which he did not return. In Poland and Lithuania, at least five of Julien's aunts and uncles were also murdered.

The *Serpa Pinto*, a Portuguese ship, took the Studleys to Havana. The cabins below decks were so unappetizing that the family elected to stay on deck in the open air for the entire 20-day trip. Maria was seasick the whole time. The ship arrived in Havana in March 1942. The Studley brothers were enrolled in school, which they both remember to be lax in discipline and academically undemanding. "I just copied the textbook," says George. "I was teased by the other kids—they'd call out 'Polago, polago!' If you were from Europe, you were a Polago and if you were American, you were a gringo." The brothers quickly became fluent in Spanish. Their father also picked up the language easily, but not Maria. "She knew that basura meant trash," says George. "Not much more than that."

Cuba felt "like heaven" to Julien. "We'd left a highly threatening environment and arrived in a place where everyone was friendly," he explains. "We were different, of course. But Cubans identified you according to economic standards, not because you were Jewish."

Julien's high school was shut down in early 1943 by a student strike protesting corruption in Cuba's educational establishment. "I had nothing to do," says Julien, "and we had no money because my father wasn't permitted to work. So I learned how to cut and polish diamonds." The training was provided by Belgian Jews who had fled to Havana from the diamond center of Antwerp at the beginning of the war. At age 15, Julien was soon earning money to help out the family. He has been working ever since.

Julien first tasted Zionism in Cuba. "I got involved with a militant youth group. They were scornful of American Jews who supported a Jewish homeland in Palestine but were never going to settle there themselves. They called those so-called Zionists 'export Jews.'" Julien even felt the influence of a religious Zionist group called Hashomer HaDati, meaning "keeper of the religion." "It gave me an identity," says Julien. "I started to have feelings about religion. I remember coming home one day during Passover, and criticizing my mother for making rice. Like leavened bread, it was considered by my new friends to be forbidden at Passover." That was a brief phase for Julien, who never again showed interest in religious ritual. After attending a graduation exercise for his son, Jacob, at the University of Chicago in 2001, Julien voiced strong unhappiness that all attending had been asked to stand for an opening prayer. For Julien, graduation was no place for religious ritual.

At the end of 1943, less than two years after their arrival in Cuba, the family received visas to come to America through relatives in New York. Lurking German submarines made the passage between Cuba and Florida perilous, so the family flew to Miami aboard a DC-3. The Studley's year and a half of safety in Cuba corresponded to a ghastly period of deportations of Jews from Western Europe, including 40,000 from France alone. In Belgium, the number of deportees reached 15,000.

The Studleys reached New York in December 1943. They camped out in the West End Avenue apartment of Solomon Melup and his family. They had last seen him boarding a ship in Bayonne. After several weeks, the family rented an apartment on West 82nd Street—their fourth household in four countries in four years. Max got a job with Bristol Instrument Company, a maker of industrial control equipment based in Waterbury, Connecticut. His assignment, in this period before the end of the real war and the onset of the Cold War, was to prepare a Russian language catalog of Bristol products and to handle contacts with Soviet customers. The commute between Manhattan and Waterbury was lengthy, and Max returned home only on weekends.

George was admitted to the High School of Music and Art after submitting a drawing portfolio and singing the Marseillaise "as a soprano." He was soon failing almost all his subjects. Partly, that might have been due to his as yet rudimentary English. But George claims he even flunked French, his native language. Julien defends his brother's academics: "He can't have done that badly, or how could he have gone on to graduate from City College?"

For Julien, who became a New Yorker at age 16, three years older than his brother, the timing was all wrong for schooling. In a split with his wife, Max did not push Julien to be a student. "My father pointed out that his own good education hadn't helped him prosper in the world. Our relatives without education were better off."

So Julien went directly to work polishing diamonds. "It was disgusting work," says George, who sometimes helped his brother in the shop after school. "You had this series of spinning wheels, like phonographs, which you rubbed with diamond paste. The stone was held with a kind of claw. More often than not, the diamond would fly off. Then it was down on all fours to find the damn thing..."

Julien acted as a contractor, cutting and polishing diamonds for their owners. Soon, he had several employees working on multiple polishing wheels in rented space at 516

Fifth Avenue. At 17, he was already a boss. "I knew I could make money in diamonds," Julien says, "but I'd always be a second class citizen because I didn't have connections. If your family wasn't already established in the business, you'd never really be accepted. Diamonds wasn't the right business for me."

With that insight, Julien gave up his own small business. He did continue to earn money processing diamonds for a firm in downtown Manhattan. His fellow workers were highly religious, and their interest in the secular world was severely limited with one exception: the great Jewish baseball player, Hank Greenberg of the Detroit Tigers. "It was amazing how much these Hasidim knew about the game," says Julien.

Julien admits that he "felt a little bit lost in America." Not that he or anyone in the family had time to reflect. "We were all scrambling to survive," he says. One evening, he attended a performance at the old Madison Square Garden of Ben Hecht's *A Flag is Born*, a rousing Zionist review in which the role of an ardent young Jewish patriot was played by an unknown but magnetic newcomer named Marlon Brando.

As Julien left the theater, he agreed to be signed up by agents in the lobby as a volunteer for the American League for a Free Palestine. The group was actually a front for the Irgun, the small, secretive, fiercely militant fighting organization led by Menachem Begin. Like the mainstream Haganah, the Irgun was fighting for a Jewish state in Palestine. Unlike the Haganah, the Irgun was uncompromising in its attitude toward both the British and the Arabs. In 1947, the Irgun showed what it thought of the British by blowing up their headquarters in a wing of the King David Hotel in Jerusalem, killing 17 people.

George also joined the Irgun. "As the little brother, either I had to be brought in or be killed," he jokes. The brothers were sent for training to a Massachusetts farm belonging to a graphics designer named Nathan Horowitz. Julien was assigned to do recruiting while George was involved with secretly collecting weapons to send to Palestine. "I went with a few guys who were packing weapons into a garage under West 155th Street one night," says George. "The cops suddenly arrived and we spent the night in jail. In the morning, my father arrived with three cronies with whom he'd been playing cards. But it was Paul O'Dwyer who liberated us." O'Dwyer, then a labor leader, lawyer, and brother of a New York City mayor, would later serve as Manhattan borough president. Why did the high profile O'Dwyer involve himself with a couple of teenagers in an obscure Zionist organization?

"As an Irish patriot, anything that was anti-British he would do," answers George.

After a year serving the American League for a Free Palestine, Julien was asked if he wanted to join the Irgun. "I was sent to an address on Minetta Lane in Greenwich Village," remembers Julien. "I entered an apartment with a curtain drawn across the middle of the living room. In front was a table on which were a gun and a bible"

"Are you ready to join the Irgun?" said a voice from the other side of the curtain.

Julien was ready.

"From this day on," said the voice, "you will be called 'Dov.'" (Dov is Hebrew for bear.)

The brothers plunged deeper into Irgun actions. As the newly declared state of Israel fought for its existence against combined Arab armies in the spring of 1948, the Irgun outfitted a supply ship, the *Altalena,* which was to sail from Port de Bouc, near Marseilles, to Israel in support of its military effort. As the *Altalena* approached Tel Aviv, it was stuffed with 800 volunteers as well as with armament. When Begin, leader of a breakaway militia, refused Ben Gurion's demand to turn over control of the *Altalena's* cargo to the newborn state, the strong-willed prime minister ordered the ship to be bombed after most on board were evacuated. The *Altalena,* and its cargo of arms, sunk on June 21, 1948.

The Irgun continued to harass the British. In New York, Julien and George did their part in the effort, carrying out assignments that they refuse to talk about to this day. Begin trusted the Studley brothers enough to assign them to guard his room at the Chatham Hotel during a visit to New York. He did not forget them. Forty years later, as Israel's prime minister, he awarded them medals for service to the state.

Julien's service to the Irgun seems out of character. His politics are leftist and, in business dealings, his ability to diffuse confrontations and still get things done is legendary. So why the gun-toting, British-whacking Irgun? "To establish the state of Israel, you needed some drastic action," Julien explains. "The Irgun was one of the most effective tools to make that happen. Compared to the Irgun, the Haganah was a bunch of fuddy-duddies." After that teenaged embrace,

Julien distanced himself from Zionist politics, which, he says, "became too intensely disputatious for my taste."

So, at the age when others had just graduated from high school, Julien was already retired from the diamond business as well as from service as a Zionist militant. What would be his next career direction?

The answer to that question was revealed to Julien through an issue of *Life* magazine dated October 28, 1946. It contained a profile of 41-year-old William Zeckendorf, a theatrical, cigar-chomping mogul who was the driving force behind a real estate company called Webb & Knapp. Zeckendorf was a master juggler with deals always in the air, but what really fascinated Julien about this impresario was his assemblage of six midtown blocks along the East River. The area had long festered with steamy tenements and slaughterhouses. Zeckendorf's original intent was to develop a futuristic neighborhood on the site with extensions thrusting into the river. Instead, John D. Rockefeller Jr. would purchase the site in 1947 for $8.5 million and donate it to the United Nations as a permanent home.

A hybrid of the chess board and the poker table, as Zeckendorf played it, the game of commercial real estate would also be Julian's calling. But before becoming its master, he would become an American in his head and heart. And for Julien, that happened when he became a soldier.

3 Army Days

Being a leader doesn't mean being first in line for lunch. It means being last in line or maybe not eating at all.

—Julien Studley

At age 24, Julien had been jolted aplenty by life—but nothing, in his own mind, quite compared with being drafted into the army in the fall of 1950. Upon reporting to Fort Lee in Ayer, Massachusetts, he was assigned to the 278th Regimental Combat Team of the Tennessee National Guard. Julien was an extra body needed to bring the unit up to full strength prior to being shipped off to the Korean combat zone.

Julien had never met a "hillbilly," let alone a whole unit of fellows whom, he jokes, "had one leg shorter than the other from walking the hillsides." No doubt Julien was equally strange to the Tennesseans. "I had to explain to them my background, what it meant to be a refugee," he says. Despite their differences, the hillbillies and the refugee got along well. Julien was soon teaching a class of 10 students in spoken Russian. "They picked it up very well, especially those who were musicians," he says. "We had fun together."

As a lowly recruit, Julien "just worked at being a soldier, getting up at six o'clock reveille, shivering in the morning formation, taking my gun apart, crawling under barbed wire with things exploding around me." Julien's MOS (military occupation specialty) was to be a mortar fire spotter. This required stationing himself high in a tree carrying a listening device. Hearing the thud of enemy mortar fire, he and two partners, staked out in other trees, would triangulate on the source of the incoming round.

"Had I not been agile in trees," says Julien. "This specialty would probably have meant my death." A sergeant who had taken Julien's Russian language class had a better idea. "He advised me to take the tests for psychological warfare, which required knowing the language of the enemy," explains Julien. "This was the Cold War, and we had a fear that the Russians were coming. In psychological warfare, you wanted to find out what would make enemy troops lay down their arms, how to make them question obedience to their leaders."

Private Studley passed army language exams in French, Spanish, German, Russian, and Polish. Despite being strongly recommended for transfer to psychological warfare, he was cautioned not to count on it actually happening. "Infantry had priority because of the fighting in Korea," Julien says. "The Pentagon told me told me that my papers for a transfer to psychological warfare would probably get lost—unless I could get my congressman to write a letter to the army personnel director on my behalf."

Julien didn't know his congressman, but he did know "a girl named Chickie" who had been a secretary to Guy M. Gillette, president of the American League for a Free Palestine. Gillette, a former senator from Iowa, had taken that job during an interval out of office. When he was later reelected to the senate, Chickie had gone to work for him on Capitol Hill. Julien paid a call on Chickie. Could she arrange for the senator to write a letter recommending Julien for assignment to psychological warfare?

"Sure, I'll do it for you right now," answered Chickie, turning to her typewriter. Julien was startled to see her write and sign the letter herself with the senator's name. This was normal procedure, Chickie assured Julien. It saved the senator's time for more important matters.

Julien returned to Fort Lee just as several units, including his own, were ordered to Korea. Another unit was posted to duty guarding aircraft at a military airfield in Iceland. The soldiers were given a week's furlough before departing. At roll call, Julien told his sergeant that he was expecting orders to be transferred to psychological warfare.

"Maybe so," said the sergeant, "but your MOS has priority because of the war." Then he added, "The army doesn't care who goes to Korea, so long as the quota gets filled. They just want warm bodies. I'll ask for volunteers who have your MOS. There are guys here who can't wait to be sprung."

Two soldiers volunteered to ship out in Julien's place. "I still remember their names," says Julien says. "Tommie Tigue and Bob Cucinella."

Julien was transferred to Fort Riley, Kansas, where the 301st Radio Broadcasting and Leaflet Group, based in Manhattan, had recently been activated. It was, as Julien quickly discovered, one of the army's most offbeat units. A soldier getting a medical discharge, whose bunk Julien was inheriting, tossed a book his way. "Read this," he said. It was *Darkness at Noon*, Arthur Koestler's classic novel of disillusionment with Stalinism. "In most army units," says Julien, "I would have been tossed a comic book or maybe a Mickey Spillane whodunit." The 301st was certainly different. "We had a pair of cousins," says Julien, "who would entertain themselves on marches during basic training by playing mental chess. They kept track of the board and the positions of all its pieces in their heads."

The mission of the 301st was propaganda. The unit was staffed with writers, illustrators, broadcasters, printers, radio technicians, translators, historians, and political scientists who were trained to pierce the Iron Curtain with anticommunist broadsides. A few blocks from where Julien had toiled in rented space as a diamond processor, the 301st's Manhattan-based reservists regularly met at the NBC building in glamorous Rockefeller Center.

The two worlds could not have been farther apart. The 301st's ranks were peppered with young NBC executives and pages. The *New York Daily News* supplied printers. The first commander of the 301st, Colonel Gruber, was the civilian boss of the *News*'s printing division. Headquarters company, to which Julien was attached, was led by Lieutenant Joseph Medill Patterson Jr., a West Pointer whose family owned both the *Chicago Tribune* and the *New York Daily News*. In the army pecking order, the patrician newspaper owner was subordinate to the printer. Mel Juffe, a journalist for the Newark-based *Star-Ledger* and a writer with the 301st's leafleting group, remembers that Patterson told the group, "Gather around me, boys, because my voice isn't too loud." A decade earlier, the editorial voice of the family newspapers had been shrill in its isolationism. Only the Japanese attack on Pearl Harbor changed that stance.

Few reservists in the 301st anticipated that their unit, with its focus on Eastern Europe, would be activated for duty in Korea. They did not have the language skills to create anti-North Korean or anti-Chinese propaganda. Still, the 301st found itself sent to basic training at Fort Riley, Kansas, in the summer of 1951. That season would be remembered as the "summer of heat and floods." The Mississippi River rose so high that July that, for a time, Fort Riley was isolated by flood waters. Only the 301st's radio transmitter was beaming to the outside world. While awaiting overseas orders at Fort Riley, the unit produced a series of leaflets meant to incite sabotage among communist-held prisoners and to encourage their hopes for freedom.

The 301st supplemented basic training with lectures by experts on newspaper publishing, European politics, and history. For Julien, it was a pleasure to be in the classroom again for the first time since his Havana high school had been closed down by student strikers. Though far from home, Julien even managed to rendezvous with his brother. George Studley was then an enlistee in the air force, stationed at an Idaho air base. They met for dinner, one Passover, at the Brown Palace, Denver's best hotel.

In late autumn of 1951, the 301st departed for Germany. Crossing the Atlantic on a troop ship in November, the unit's literary lions entertained the other soldiers aboard by staging nine performances of an original revue called "Knots to You." A cold rain fell and a military band played as the ship docked in Bremerhaven. The unit went by train to the village of Kafertal, just outside Mannheim. The troops were housed in a former Wehrmacht facility, renamed the Sullivan barracks. "We were issued carbines," says Mel Juffe, "but they were kept locked up so we wouldn't hurt ourselves." Juffe was also amazed at the handsome, high urinals in the facility. He speculates that "they were designed for some race of superman, like Hitler dreamed of."

The soldiers of the 301st were not supermen, but neither was their army world quite ordinary. Julien found this out one Friday evening, when another G.I. from the headquarters company, Gates Davison, asked him about his weekend plans. Julien had none.

"So come with me on a little excursion," said Davison.

They drove to a large, gated house in Bonn, where an army guard peered at Davison and welcomed him by name. A movie was being shown in a screening room in the house. Gates and friend took seats in the darkness. When the lights came up, a handsome woman offered the soldiers homemade cookies. She was the wife of John J. McCloy, the U.S. High Commissioner and governor of Occupied Germany, and it was here in their residence that Julien spent the weekend.

McCloy was related to Davison's family, which had been a founder of the Morgan Bank. "Davison's character references for the army," says Julien, "were two secretaries of state, Dean Acheson and John Foster Dulles." Julien remembers seeing on Davison's desk an invitation to the summer home in Normandy of the American ambassador to Paris. "I was amazed to meet a person who had access to almost anyone who had power," says Julien. "These people could push buttons and make things happen based on their class." They had a network. But their power was on the way out. When Gates died, years later, his estate left some paintings, but he had run out of money."

The 301st was the sole psychological warfare group in Europe, and one of only two in the army. Why were they called the 301st? "We wanted to frighten the enemy," cracks Mel Juffe, "by making them think there were 300 units like ours ready to bury them in insults." Behind the joking, according to Alan Bandler, another New Yorker in the unit, "there was a genuine fear that the Soviet army would attempt to overrun Europe. In case of an attack, we'd probably have been moved back to Paris to protect our radio transmitter."

So long as there was no war, the 301st was not permitted to leaflet or broadcast behind the Iron Curtain. It served by waiting. "We could do whatever we wanted, because nobody knew what we were supposed to do," says Juffe, who edited the group's quasi-literary magazine, called *Psyche.* Typical of its cheeky style, a review in the first issue (dated December, 1952) dismissed a book of essays on modern France as "a painless way to become familiar with such concepts as the French *élan vital* and the Third Force as well as top personalities and everything else that's wrong with France." A later issue spoofed Socratic dialogue (Norman Rappaport, a printer from Brooklyn, became a character named Rappaplato).

Although the 301st might not have excelled in a shooting war, it was hard to beat at snappy verse, such as these lines about the unit in *Psyche*:

Our army has something it's not had before,
Its tactics have turned pedagogical;
This new kind of fighting is labeled PsyWar
But it's somewhat more psycho than logical.
In the past our men knew the meaning of strife,
Each man was well-armed and a killer
But he fought with a Mauser or Luger or knife
Not a page out of Goethe or Schiller.

Soon after his arrival at Sullivan barracks, Julien was attending a Russian language class when an officer entered and asked if anyone had civilian "business" clothes. Since soldiers could only leave the base in uniform, "civvies" were scarce. Julien, who did happen to have a sportscoat and slacks, found himself on temporary assignment to a unit identified only as Detachment R. It was based in Regensberg in eastern Germany, near the Czech border. The mission of Detachment R (for Russian) was to be a school for intelligence about the Soviets and their satellites. Its students were Soviet security specialists from U.S. intelligence services. Their teachers were anticommunist Russian defectors, "people we'd found in Germany when we got there in the mid-1940s," says Julien. In their courses, the teachers dissected the strengths and weaknesses of the Soviet Union not as academics, although some of them were, but as insiders.

"My orders were to get to know these faculty members and critique a new course they were developing on psychological warfare," explains Julien, who insisted he was unqualified for this assignment but was told to proceed as ordered. "I also compiled a report on how each of these defectors might help us in case of a hot war. I remember, especially, the words of a Chechen professor: 'I see the eventual disintegration of the USSR arising out of the problem of unresolved nationalities.' Fifty years later, as the professor predicted, the Soviet empire had disintegrated and Russians and Chechens were killing each other over the issue of unresolved nationalities."

Except for Julien, all other American military personnel in Detachment R were officers of field grade (major or higher). "The others couldn't figure out who I was, but personal probing was not welcomed in the atmosphere of this place," he says. "I'd arrived with another fellow, a lieutenant. I think they suspected I was an intelligence official and he was my aide de camp." Julien did good work at Detachment R and soon received another temporary assignment to a defector reception facility (DRF) directed by U.S. intelligence agencies in the spa resort of Wiesbaden. The center was pleasingly housed in a compound of villas overlooking the Rhine.

Deep-mining his language skills, Julien debriefed defectors from Czechoslovakia, Poland, Romania, Hungary, and a few from Russia. Unlike Detachment R's hard-core, early defecting anticommunists, the Russian defectors at the DRF "had just crossed over to our side of the Iron Curtain to get out of trouble," explains Julien. "Maybe they'd gotten drunk and crashed an army vehicle. They were afraid of the consequences if they'd stayed."

Each defector was assigned a nominal "sponsor" who, says Julien, "was really a guard." Debriefing required patience, and could go on for months. Rather than elicit military intelligence, Julien's job—"I was very focused on it"—was to coax out "songs, jokes, and mishaps" which the Voice of America could use to ring bells of authenticity in its broadcasts to communist countries. Julien's reports were returned to him with the most useful portions underlined. Listening to Voice of America broadcasts, he could sometimes hear his best material beamed through the Iron Curtain.

"I didn't speak all the languages of the defectors," says Julien, "but there was always a way to be understood. The Czechs knew some German or Russian, the Poles could get by in Russian, the Hungarians in German, and most Romanians knew French." In whatever language, Julien took nothing that was said at face value. "If you only listened to their words, you would miss out on what they were really thinking. They only used the words that they thought you wanted to hear. You had to see through the smoke and mirrors." Although a nonsmoker and not much of a drinker while off duty, Julien didn't hesitate to light up with his subjects and, if it loosened up their tongues, bring out a bottle of cognac. "The only way to go was gently," he says.

Later, as a CEO, Julien deployed his interviewing skills toward real estate brokers as subtlety as he once did with defectors—never more so than when he decided in 2001 to step into a festering dispute between two successful brokers who had a falling out after being partners in Studley's Atlanta office. In the aftermath of the feud, one broker had relocated to the Washington office. He claimed that, under an agreement with his former partner, he was entitled to split any commission on deals that arose out of client contacts made in the previous two years when the partnership was still functioning. If he didn't get what he wanted, the broker was threatening to quit the company and sue for commission shares he claimed were due him.

The dispute was already being arbitrated internally, as per company policy, by a senior officer. But when the unhappy broker resisted settlement, Julien decided to intervene. That did not sit well with the arbitrator, who told Julien that it would compromise his own authority if Julien settled the dispute.

"I don't want to settle it," said Julien. "I want to defuse it."

The broker was called to New York for a meeting with Julien that began in his corner office. It was a situation ripe for confrontation, but Julien hoped that he could avoid that. "This broker was unbelievably competitive physically," he says. "So when he came in the office, prepared for a fight, I steered him into talking about the triathlon races he participated in with his wife, who may have been even more fit than he was. We talked like that for about an hour. And then I could see that he was starting to unwind."

That was when Julien abruptly switched the subject and fired an unexpected salvo with pinpoint aim: "Have you ever read your employment contract to learn what happens to an employee who separates from the company?"

"Ummm... I don't exactly remember what the contract says."

"You signed it. It says you're not entitled to any commission cuts after one year. And we protected you for that year."

While Julien let his words sink in, he again shifted gears, this time downshifting the tension: "By the way, we're having a break for our Kris Kringle party. Why don't you come join us? The office does this every year before Christmas."

Gift giving at the Kris Kringle party is based on random name drawing. "What makes it a nice event," explains Julien, "is the $20 limit on gifts. That forces you to think of what the other person might really like to get. This broker stood aside at first, but as I introduced him to people he hadn't met, he sort of got into the spirit of it. I noticed that he seemed to really like a pair of fuzzy socks that was my gift to someone." Platters of sushi had been set out, along with holiday cookies, but the broker from Washington showed no interest.

"Have you ever tried sushi?" asked Julien.

"Never."

"Try a little, it's not so bad. It's health food."

The broker took a tentative taste and conceded that, by golly, it wasn't so bad. He rather liked it.

"When you go back to Washington," said Julien, "go to Steve [Stephen Goldstein, head of the Washington office, was the arbitrator] and surprise him by saying, 'Steve, let's go out and have sushi.' Then I sent him a pair of the fuzzy socks."

It could have been a screaming match, followed by calling in the lawyers, precisely the scenario Julien was determined to head off. Still, along with the banter, the Kris Kringle party, the sushi, and the fuzzy socks, Julien had reminded the broker of his precise contractual responsibilities to the firm. True to his word, Julien had not settled the dispute. He had defused it.

While Julien shuttled between Detachment R and the defector reception center, he always returned to the Sullivan barracks, where he took his turn at guard duty—even though, as his buddy Alan Bandler insists, "the only people who wanted to infiltrate our base were German prostitutes." Evenings in the barracks, Bandler remembers, would bring on lively conversation among "guys who wore smoking jackets and slippers and smoked pipes. It was strange, knowing that 10 thousand miles away, other G.I.'s were being killed in Korea."

On the surface, Julien's army experience appeared to be identical to that of his buddies. But only on the surface. For the others, the army was an interval in a firmly grounded life. Julien's life had been filled with dislocations. The family had escaped Hitler by a hairbreadth. He'd attended schools in three countries, none of them American, and made it to high school only to see the students close it down. The one job he'd actually trained for in Havana turned out to be remote from his true learnings, which were more toward bringing out the best in people rather than in diamonds. In New York, he'd pledged to militant Zionism as a teenager, yet he had no wish to emigrate to Israel. Entering the army, Julien admitted to still feeling "a little bit lost."

But two years as a G.I. merged Julien into the mainstream of his new country. Interacting with his own buddies and with diverse Europeans, he had a chance to cultivate his formidable "people" strengths. He would make up for youthful friendships lost to instability by holding fast to army friendships for the rest of his life. Above all, Julien used those two years to plant his two feet firmly on American earth that would not again move out from under him.

After being honorably discharged, Julien received a letter from the 301st, dated November 3, 1952, telling him that it had heard from "the gentleman for whom you worked on your last assignment. Unfortunately, military security prevents us from either sending you the letter or identifying the source, but he would like you to know how highly he thought of your... tact, diplomacy, initiative and dispatch."

Fresh out of the army, Julien applied for a job with the CIA, but despite his relevant experience and the unnamed gentleman's good words, he was rejected.

Julien had begun his real estate career, before army service, as a self-described "energetic foreigner." "But when I came back to New York," he says. "I felt that I had done good things for my country."

Julien also came out of the army with his high school equivalency certificate. "My mother had been displeased when I went to work instead of finishing high school after our arrival from Cuba," he says. "When I showed her the certificate, she was happy."

4 Starting Studley

If I had gone to business school, I'd probably now have a much larger company—or I'd be bankrupt.

—Julien Studley

Julien was 19 years old when he read about developer William Zeckendorf Jr. in *Life* magazine. "Not since Napoleon III redesigned the city of Paris in the 1850s has anybody indulged a more grandiose appetite for real estate than a Manhattan operator named Zeckendorf," said the article.

The world of high-stakes real estate fired up Julien's imagination in a way that diamonds had not. Lacking contacts in this world, he got a list of member firms from the Real Estate Board of New York and began looking for a job as a trainee. Interviewed at the old-line brokerage of Brett Wycoff Potter Hamilton, Julien was asked if he could speak Yiddish. He had picked up a smattering of the language, while working in the diamond trade. That would be helpful in dealing with clients in the polyglot garment center. Julien got the job, but with this caveat from Mr. Hamilton, the interviewer: "Before you come to work, polish your shoes."

Julien augmented his paltry earnings by moonlighting as a diamond polisher. He continued living in the family apartment at 640 Riverside Drive and gave all his earnings to his mother, who doled out what little pocket cash he needed. Julien also continued to be a Zionist activist, briefly dating Janet Berley, another young volunteer at the American League for a Free Palestine. "She took cabs, and I was a subway guy," says Julien, and they did not date for long.

In 1949 Julien joined Berley & Company, the real estate firm owned by Janet's family. He was put under the wing of a broker specializing in renting space to printing firms, which required industrial-strength buildings and long leases because the weight and size of their presses made moving a major effort. Julien soon moved to L.V. Hoffman Inc., a specialist in loft brokerage. "Hoffman was not as classy as Berley," says Julien. But it did pay him $50 a week to start, a sum which Julien calls, in that era of nickel subway tokens, "pretty close to respectable."

Civilian life was interrupted, in the spring of 1950, by Julien's sojourn in the army. Two years later, he returned to L.V. Hoffman with a new level of self-confidence instilled by his service as a psychological warrior. Although becoming a mini-Zeckendorf was not his aim, Julien was ready to move upward as he learned about leasing. Like most so-called brokers, Julien was licensed only as a real estate salesperson. He could strike a deal, but the commission agreement only could be signed by a person holding a broker's license. It was always somebody else who sealed the deal. "Old man Hoffman didn't want his people getting broker's licenses," says Mike Solomon, who was also a junior salesperson with L.V. Hoffman. "He thought he could control things more tightly by only having licensed sales people."

Julien pleads a poor memory for names, but he does not forget addresses. He can still tick off those of his workaday deals at L.V. Hoffman—18 East 18th Street, 13 East 15th Street, 16 East 17th Street—and his "pride and joy, a 50-footer with two elevators at 87 Fifth Avenue," for which he was the exclusive rental agent.

At 40 Union Square West, Julien remembers trying to do a deal with a certain Mr. Tisch, who was a garment cutter. "Cutters were a rather big deal," says Julien, "because you could ruin a lot of fabric in one cut if you did it wrong." (Mr. Tisch's children and grandchildren became even more powerful through the growth of the family business, which became Loews Corporation.) "I asked Mr. Tisch about a photo of a hotel on the wall of his office," says Julien. 'Oh, that's Laurel-in-the-Pines in New Jersey,' he answered. 'My family manages it.' Laurel-in-the-Pines was the first Loews hotel."

Months after his return from the military, Julien was fired by L.V. Hoffman for failing to follow company rules. "It was something that I could have fixed," says Julien, "but this was an opportunity. L.V. Hoffman was no longer the place for me once I got out of the army. I wanted to get out on my own." Six months after being fired, Julien was licensed as a real estate broker.

At age 27, Julien moved out of his family's apartment on Riverside Drive into a one-bedroom, fourth-floor walk-up at 400 East 53rd Street, a building that was managed by L.V. Hoffman—a move that his family was against. George was especially hurt, swearing he'd never again speak to his big brother. Max Studley, ever the classical music buff, typed up a departure list of recommended recordings for Julien. In French, it was organized under the headings "chamber music, symphonic music, opera, masses, and oratories." The new apartment became the first office of Julien J. Studley, Inc., incorporated in December 1954. Early the next year, Mike Solomon bumped into Julien in the street. "He said, 'Hey, I'm taking 400 square feet at 424 Madison Avenue. Do you want to join me?'" "The guy had nothing to his name," says Solomon. "But even then, he gave you a feeling of confidence." Solomon left L.V. Hoffman to join Julien and stayed for almost 50 years.

"Somehow," says Solomon, "I think that back then, people my age relied more on serendipity than any kind of career planning. It was a question of watching World War II go by and seeing all those people die, and then the Korean War. We were more casual about our lives. Today, people are a lot more studied."

Julien had a hunch that his future would not be in loft rentals, where he had experience, but in office leasing. On the map of commercial brokerage, office leasing was then hardly more than a dot, but Julien's timing was on the money. The last great office building boom had ended by 1931 with a flourish of midtown landmark towers including the Chrysler, Empire State, Lincoln, McGraw-Hill, Daily News buildings, and 500 Fifth Avenue. Except for the creation of Rockefeller Center, construction went dead until 1947, when the Tishman family built 445 Park Avenue, a 22-floor, 316,000-square-foot tower at 57th Street. In 1951, came Lever House, the first of the curtain-wall towers, designed by Gordon Bunshaft, and freshly agleam for the new millennium after a painstaking renovation. The staid apartment buildings and hotels along Park Avenue north of Grand Central Station up to 60th Street yielded to a march of new office towers. One of them, the Colgate-Palmolive Building at 300 Park Avenue, was under construction as Julien started his business in 1954. Thirty years later, the building's third floor became Studley's national headquarters.

All this new office construction—32 million square feet in 92 buildings between 1954 and 1960—should have meant booming business for Julien's new firm. There was only one problem: Few if any of the tower owners, among them the Tishman, Uris, Durst, and Fisher families, had heard of Studley. Their business went to entrenched commercial brokers like Cross & Brown, Charles Noyes, Cruickshank, Cushman & Wakefield, and Helmsley-Spear. "The old-line firms were tied to the landlords, so the path of least resistance was to represent tenants," says David Raspler, a broker who joined Studley in the late 1950s. "In a strong market, landlords came to the table with the upper hand. The tenant came naked. This was the key to establishing ourselves. We represented the user. This is where the opening was. It was a radical choice we made, but logical."

That summer of 1954, Studley became a force of two with the arrival of Hy Gross, his partner in owning an old rear-engine Mercedes in their army days in Germany. Gross stayed a few years before heading off to law school. Then came Mel Wolfe, recommended by Julien's friend, Betsy Sanders. Wolfe introduced Julien to the New York City Ballet, which became a lifelong love. Mike Solomon was the fourth to arrive, just after Studley moved to its new space at 424 Madison Avenue in 1955. He remembers that "the office was divided in two, with Julien, Hy, and Mel at the three desks along with a receptionist." The firm became the agent for several small office buildings, including the former Hotel Fairfax at 65 East 55th Street. "There was a fashion to convert hotels to offices then," says Julien. This work meant representing owners rather than tenants, but the firm was in no condition to be choosy. "I wasn't thinking of gold," says Julien, "only of survival."

Survival thinking didn't mean restricted thinking. In the year that Julien started his business, he decided that he could do more for his tenant clients by offering them interior design services as well as office space. With Jack Freidin, a young architect who had worked in the office of Bauhaus luminary Marcel Breuer, he formed Freidin-Studley Associates. "I felt early on that you can't separate leasing space from designing space," says Julien. "Each building lays out differently, and to really know what a tenant needed, you had to do plans. Jack would sketch out ideas at client meetings. It got us into the whole art of presentation." If the leasing client liked the design, Jack would negotiate a fee for the installation. A high point of the collaboration was Frieden-Studley's design for Aeronaves de Mexico at 500 Fifth Avenue in 1957. Its south-of-the-border ambiance featured a large, scary-looking, Aztec-style statue in the recessed, red-brick-paved office entrance. The interior balanced traditional crafts with sleek, modernist furniture and lighting.

Freidin-Studley Associates was a rather grand title for a firm in which the architect kept his day job and moonlighted at the Studley office. "Julien was always good at making the company look bigger than it really was when it was young," says Stanley Kovak, who joined the firm in the mid-1960s. Freidin was also young, and glad to get the extra work. He soon opened his own practice specializing in office interiors, including the New York headquarters of Playboy Inc. in its prime and the newsroom of *The New York Times.* "Interiors are more complex to design than exteriors," said Freiden in an interview shortly before his death from cancer in 2004. "Flows of people and their placement take more thought than a façade. You have to analyze the business in order to get it right."

Friedin-Studley's design services were billed to the client, with a payback: The standard 40 percent discount architects received for ordering furniture was passed through to the client in outfitting the new office. There was also a bonus in design currency for Julien: "This was my first foray into architecture. I learned a lot from Jack."

George Studley joined his big brother in the firm in 1957. "I don't know that he was all that keen on me being there," says George, "but I persuaded him." In later years, Studley would pioneer the concept of teams that provide clients with sophisticated packages of financial, tax, construction, demographic, transportation, and labor market analysis. But in the late 1950s, according to George, "being a broker was just a sales job, canvassing for leads, trying to be the guy who signed the sales agreement." Although the telephone was a tool in seeking clients, it was no substitute for a pair of sturdy shoes. David Raspler, apprenticed to George as a 21-year-old, called his only asset "my ability to outwalk anyone else." Peter

Speier, who joined the firm in 1962 (in the same week that Don Schnabel arrived), remembers his first week on the job, endlessly trudging up and down the 55 floors of Radio City and other buildings in Rockefeller Center, checking for empty offices or for signs of a tenant moving, and chatting up receptionists to pick up any extra tidbits. "If a manager or even a secretary would agree to see you, you'd have a chance. A boss could come to work that very morning realizing that the lease is up in a couple of months and he's got to do something." After two days of floor hopping, Speier was told by Raspler, "You're on your own." That was the end of his apprenticeship.

Peter Speier, destined to be a master among law firm brokers, hoped to start his career at prestigious Cushman & Wakefield. "John Cushman said he liked me, but he didn't have an extra desk," says Speier. "While waiting for my interview, I'd noticed an advertisement for Studley in a real estate magazine. Their office was only a block away at 342 Madison Avenue, so I went straight over. It turned out Julien was just moving in. I asked him how much he could pay me."

"Julien just looked at me. Finally, he said, 'What are you thinking?' It is hard for any young person starting out in brokerage to appreciate that salary is a dirty word. You get a desk and a phone and just possibly a small monthly draw against what you'll earn. A broker lives by commission."

Even in later years, when functions like budgeting and goal setting were formalized at Studley, broker training remained a loose affair. The classroom is still out there in the domain of rentable space. A trainee is put under the eye of a seasoned broker. If, by dint of charm, subterfuge, or luck, the trainee manages to get an appointment with a potential tenant, it will be the senior broker who joins him in keeping the date. If the deal is closed, the trainee shares in the commission.

Studley has nurtured many exceptional brokers, even superstars. Explaining his own absence from their pantheon, Julien says, "I discovered fairly early on that my mind is a little too split. To be a really successful broker you have to be directed down a single channel. But I'm usually looking at things in fairly multiple ways—all the pros and cons. Analyzing the options. I like to be a doubter, and that's not the way to be a great broker. On the other hand, being a doubter does work better when you're working for tenants rather than for owners. A buyer of space has more options to ponder than a seller of space, and a broker who is a doubter will think through all of them."

Not a "single channel" superbroker, perhaps, but Julien, with his broadband outlook, proved to be a gifted, albeit cautious, business builder. In 1964, a decade after the firm's birth, Studley had 15 brokers and revenues of under $2 million. Julien was then busy with the first deal that put his firm in the brokerage big leagues. After acquiring an option on the northwest corner of Third Avenue and 52nd Street, he persuaded the Tishman family, Manhattan's premier developers, to buy the entire blockfront. Tishman then erected an office tower, 866 Third Avenue, for which Studley was appointed rental agent. By the summer of 1966, the 31-floor tower was almost entirely rented (For more about this deal, see Chapter 11).

In those early days, Julien met each Friday with his press agent Gerry Freeman to discuss ways of getting the firm noticed, if possible, out of proportion to its actual size. Late in 1962, the two men had the idea of producing a monthly survey of available office space in new and upcoming office buildings. It would substitute statistics for what had previously been anecdotal information. "The philosophy was to open it all up to the public," says Julien. The first issue of the *Studley Report,* then eight typed pages, appeared in January 1963 and has been published ever since. "I stressed that we made news through providing legitimate information—real data on market conditions," says Freeman. "The only problem was that landlords with a load of empty space didn't appreciate it seeing it detailed in the Studley Report. They complained to Julien that tenants shouldn't know when they were dying. It hurt their ability to make deals on their terms. Meanwhile, no journalist could write a story on office leasing without invoking the Studley report. It got us a tremendous amount of notice. Now everyone and his brother does a market survey, but we pioneered it."

The mantra of growth for its own sake was never chanted at Studley, but opportunities were seized. In 1961, when a Chicago owner wanted a New York slant on renting up an office building, Julien dispatched a broker named Ed Aubry to open the firm's first branch office there. A few years later, Peter Speier left New York to open a branch in Washington, D.C. His assignment was to lease up five office buildings under construction in downtown and in suburban Crystal City, adjacent to National Airport, with a total of more than 1.5 million square feet. That opportunity, too attractive to turn down, showed that tenant representation was not an inflexible Studley value. When Howard Sadowsky wanted to start a branch in Los Angeles, where there was no ready-made client, he had to lobby hard for the go-ahead. "In New

York I was just another broker," says Sadowsky. "I wanted my own shop. This was a chance to plant my own flag."

The fast track to opening a branch office in an unfamiliar city, as other firms often do it, involves the purchase of a local brokerage with ready-made expertise and a client base. That is what Cushman & Wakefield did, Julien points out, when it opened a San Francisco office. Studley's own office in that city was opened by Chris Lovell, an experienced broker with the firm, who started from scratch. And he was only given the go-ahead when he begged to do it. "Some companies operate on the 'push' principle," says Don Schnabel. "They push their people to do something. Maybe it's pushing a new computer on their desks that they never asked for. Maybe it's opening a new branch office based on decision making at the top. With us, you have to scream and yell if you want a new computer, or if you want to open a new office. You have to drag us your way. We operate on the 'pull' principle."

Howard Sadowsky arrived in Los Angeles from New York in 1971, just in time to experience a major earthquake. When he raised the unfamiliar Studley flag, his laid-back competitors hardly lifted an eye to notice. Soon, he got their attention. Four months after his arrival, Sadowsky telephoned Dick Turpin, real estate editor of the *Los Angeles Times*.

"I'm not seeing many articles about commercial real estate in the newspaper," said Sadowsky. "The stuff you're doing is all residential."

Turpin's response, according to Sadowsky, was to insist that readers weren't interested in commercial real estate coverage. "I pointed out to Turpin that you see a whole lot of office buildings in L.A.," says Sadowsky. "Maybe so, he told me, but not enough to generate advertising."

Sadowsky had a proposition for Turpin: "How about if I put together a story on office leasing? You can determine if it's appropriate to put in the newspaper." Turpin wasn't enthusiastic about that idea, but he didn't reject it. Sadowsky typed out an interview with himself, as if from the pen of Turpin, covering what he'd learned so far about Los Angeles office leasing market. His hope was that what he'd written could serve as the basis for an article in which brokers from other firms would be quoted. Instead, the article was published in the Sunday real estate section exactly as it had been pulled from Sadowsky's typewriter.

"Turpin called me a few days later and said he was getting calls from other brokers who were irate," says Sadowsky. "They wanted to know who the hell was this guy? And what did this newcomer know about the Los Angeles market?" Brokers also called Sadowsky directly to complain about his presumption. "I just told them that I'd be grateful if they could notify me of any inaccuracies they found in the article," says Sadowsky. "Suddenly, our little office was on the map."

Back in New York, Julien's focus on the firm's survival had shifted to an effort at keeping key talent. The departure of a key broker hurt Julien and spurred him into creating a partnership. Eight core brokers were made shareholders in the firm: Peter Speier, David Raspler, Howard Sadowsky, Steve Goldstein, Don Schnabel, Mike Solomon, Julien, and George Studley. "Each had the right to buy equal shares so that after eight years, they'd each own one-eighth of the company," explains Julien. "We'd each share an eighth of any profit and in a bad year put up an eighth of any loss."

A few years later, five core brokers agreed to put their commissions into a communal "pot." At year's end, its contents would be split evenly. The idea was that, given the ups and downs that are a broker's lot, the equal division of the pot would smooth out everyone's earnings. As it turned out, some brokers consistently put more in the pot than others. After a few years, the pot was shelved. But not before a year in which Peter Speier put in (uncomplainingly, according to Julien) a share so much larger than his partners that they insisted on buying him a new Mercedes Benz convertible.

By allowing his partners to buy stock, Julien had hoped to keep them aboard. But the plan produced the opposite effect on his brother. George was hurt by Julien's refusal to give him priority over the other brokers, feeling that the company should become, in effect, a family firm. If there could be a Lehman Brothers, why not a Studley Brothers? But Julien felt that it would be unfair to put his brother ahead of brokers who had preceded him. "If he had started the firm with me, it would have been different," says Julien. In 1972, George left the firm. In any case, he did not feel cut out to be a broker. "I was good at putting the deals together," he explains, "but the business was just too iffy, too aggressive, and I didn't feel like I had the people skills."

For a time after leaving Studley, George was a real estate consultant and property manager. His family also spent a year in the south of France. Then he and his wife, Helen, opened Le Columbe d'Or, a restaurant with the aura of Provence, on East 26th Street in Manhattan. Though not in a traditional neighborhood for fashionable restaurants, Le Colombe d'Or caught on quickly with a clientele eager for a taste of southern France.

Studley's continued cautious and debt-free growth in the early 1970's was a universe apart from the visionary, debt-churning style of Zeckendorf, who, in any case, had gone bankrupt. "Prudence" is a key word in describing Julien's business behavior. The one visible distinction between Studley and dozens of other mid-sized commercial brokerage firms in Manhattan was the ping pong table in the office lobby at 342 Madison Avenue. The game was "a good way to relax and be competitive," says Julien, "and such an easy thing to have available." One office wall was also reserved for a dart board, and some brokers had their own set of darts. These two recreations were augmented by a regular Wednesday evening poker game, held in Julien's office until the wee hours.

Up in Harlem, Studley sponsored a series of training seminars for aspiring black brokers. They were the brainchild of Emil Schattner, a Polish-born broker. In the early 1970s, Harlem was a dead zone for brokerage, and the seminars were typical of how Studley went its own free-form way.

Except for the relationship with Tishman at 866 Third Avenue, the firm seemed, to an outside eye, to be comfortably, permanently, a doer of modest deals. But all was not quite as casual as it seemed. Studley was then secretly engaged in a skyline-altering mission that, in its skill and scale, would have rated a tip of Zeckendorf's hat.

5 Assemblage

Our business is brains, not bricks.

—Julien Studley

Donald Schnabel compares Julien Studley to a skilled chess player, "always thinking seven moves ahead." But not even Julien could foresee the immense impact of his seemingly quixotic decision in 1967 to hire Charles McArthur, a 50-year-old Arizona native with no previous experience as a broker. Julien's partners, not least Schnabel, were befuddled. McArthur, recently divorced, was as much a stranger to Manhattan as to brokerage. In a firm that began with a Jewish nucleus, McArthur was a WASP. What was Julien thinking? He assigned the new broker-in-training to be Schnabel's assistant. "This guy was 13 years older than me," says Schnabel. "I asked Julien how he could do this to me."

But Julien proved to be multiple moves ahead. Schnabel and McArthur would make a good match personally and a grand match professionally. Thanks to a chance contact initiated by McArthur, the pair would soon undertake a deal that would go down in the annals of high-stakes real estate gamesmanship.

Charles McArthur had impressive family credentials in real estate: His father and two uncles had built the Arizona Biltmore, a landmark resort hotel on the outskirts of Phoenix. They had hired Frank Lloyd Wright to help design the hotel, which, when it opened in 1929, was tagged "Queen of the Desert." Then, according to McArthur, they had fired the headstrong young architect. McArthur's family lost title to the Arizona Biltmore in the Depression when Charles Wrigley, the Chicago chewing gum magnate who had financed it, called in the loan. "After Wright died," says McArthur, "his widow, who took over his school at Taliesen West, told the students that Wright had designed the Arizona Biltmore. But my Uncle Warren was the architect. He and his older brother Albert also designed the furniture that was much praised and is still in use." McArthur says that Wright once designed a "bootleg" home for a relative in Chicago—bootleg because Wright did it on the side while working for another firm.

McArthur commuted by train to Studley's office on Madison Avenue from Green's Farms, Connecticut—Cheever country. "One morning," says McArthur, "a guy sat next to me who I'd seen a couple of times. He mentioned he was with the Ford Foundation [headquartered on East 42nd Street near the United Nations] and they were interested in developing the area around the UN. A church over on Lexington Avenue was thinking of relocating there. The Ford guy wanted to know whether, if the church sold its Lexington Avenue property, it could clear enough money to buy a new site near the UN and build a new church."

Schnabel and McArthur examined that question for "the Ford guy." Their conclusion was negative. The proceeds from selling St. Peter's Lutheran Church, at the corner of Lexington Avenue and East 54th Street, along with five adjacent townhouses, would not cover the cost of a new site and church. Not, at any rate, if only St. Peter's was put on the market. But if other parcels adjacent to the church on Lexington Avenue were also part of a deal, that assemblage could lure a skyscraper builder. Then the property values would jump.

If St. Peter's were sold to a developer, it would not be the first time. In 1871, elders had bought a defunct Presbyterian church at the corner of 46th Street and Lexington Avenue for $12,000. Thirty-one years later, as the New York Central Railroad bought up property all around it, the congregation was offered $200,000 for its corner plot. Although they considered the price to be grossly inflated, that was Commodore Vanderbilt's affair. They took the windfall and built their splendid, triple-spired church eight blocks to the north. In the hot real estate market of 1968, would St. Peter's be tempted into another windfall if the price went high enough?

The two brokers approached Dr. Ralph Peterson, the energetic young pastor who had put new zip into St. Peter's. He had started Theater at Noon for the office workers and a jazz vespers service every Sunday. A delighted Duke Ellington donated a piano for the vesper jams. For the first time in years, church membership was rising. After its recent flirtation with moving, the church had opted to stay in the hurlyburly of midtown. Pastor Peterson summed up the new feeling by paraphrasing the Jewish theologian Abraham Joshua Heschel: "Our role is not to retreat back to the catacombs [read the sedate UN neighborhood] but to become more human in skyscrapers."

So the church would not even be tempted by what Schnabel felt was a realistic selling price of $300 per square foot, or $4.5 million for its 15,000-square-foot plot. But what about double that price? That would be achievable, in Schnabel's opinion, if the church property were the keystone of an assemblage of the Lexington Avenue frontage. A check of all the properties on the block showed that no turnovers had occurred for a decade. That meant no other assemblage was already in the works.

The two brokers broached the assemblage scenario to Pastor Peterson. "He told us to go ahead and investigate, but he wasn't guaranteeing to be part of any deal," says Schnabel. "It was a very loosey-goosey commitment."

Land assemblages in Manhattan, always a slow, secretive affair, were normally done by developers, not brokers. If Schnabel and McArthur were to attempt an assemblage, who would be their client? They posed this question to Julien Studley, who responded with a question of his own:

"Who's across the street from the church?"

"The rear of First National City Bank (now Citibank)," answered Schnabel. (The front of the bank's 40-story tower was at 399 Park Avenue.)

"Let's ask them," said Julien.

Schnabel felt that suggestion was unrealistic. "As a firm, we were little nobodies," he says. "It would be difficult to get their attention." Still, with Julien's admonition in mind that "if you don't ask, you don't get," Schnabel appointed his partner to approach Citibank.

McArthur "cold-called" the bank's real estate department. Low-keyed and soft-spoken, with a touch of cowboy drawl, he succeeded in getting an appointment. The first meeting was held on the ground floor of the bank. In September 1968, after three months of lower-level discussions, Schnabel and McArthur met a senior vice president named Bob Graham. He cautiously authorized the brokers to attempt the assemblage on Lexington Avenue.

As for why the bank wanted the block, it admitted to needing more space. But a deeper reason may have been left unsaid. In recent years, Citibank had surpassed the Chase Manhattan bank in size, profits, and general oomph. Yet it had no architectural showpiece to rival Chase Manhattan Plaza downtown, with its playful Jean Dubuffet sculpture on its ample plaza and its Isamu Noguchi–sculpted courtyard. By comparison, Citibank's existing headquarters on Park Avenue was standard issue, although when it was sold at the end of 2002, it fetched over $1 billion.

In June 1969, what Julien describes as a "straightforward, almost primitive" contract was drawn up. It provided for a regular commission on each parcel on the block that was acquired. If the initial spadework indicated that the assemblage was not feasible, the bank would pay Studley a research fee for its effort.

Secrecy had to be absolute. A speculative developer could always go somewhere else if an assemblage bogged down, but the bank wanted to be directly across the street. Both parties agreed to minimize the number of people aware of the project. That was easy enough at Studley's 60-person office, where all decisions led to Julien. But, astonishingly in a publicly owned company of 17,000 employees, not more than half a dozen at the bank would ever hear about the assemblage, even as more than $25 million was spent on land alone.

Schnabel now set up a company called Lexman Realty with himself as vice president and Julien as president. That was public record. The name of Lexman's sole shareholder, the bank, was not.

Now Schnabel was ready to make his first probe on the block. Where should it be? Getting the Lexington Avenue frontage was a must. But land cost would also be highest on the avenue. Why gamble so high so soon? The probe would best be made on 53rd or 54th Streets.

Schnabel's eye settled on 139 East 53rd Street, a shoddy four-story building whose ground floor the restaurateur Roger Chauveron had elevated to what some followers of haute cuisine called glory. It had not been easy for Café Chauveron. Most of the city's great French restaurants—there were no other kinds of great restaurants then—were located in the narrow luxury band between Park and Madison. Here, east of Lexington, the Blarney Stone next door hardly helped. By hard work alone Chauveron had made his success. Schnabel did not expect him to give it up easily. However, in fact, this restaurant, along with several other spare-nothing counterparts—was not in the best financial shape. It took only one meeting with the proprietor and his accountant partner Albert Kaiser to determine that Café Chauveron's lease could be bought out. Now Schnabel approached the owner of the building, a broker named Votigliano.

"Sorry," Votigliano said, shaking his head. "I just made a contract to sell already."

"May I ask with whom?"

"A fellow named Manny Duell."

Schnabel paid a visit to Duell's tiny office on Park Avenue. A paunchy man with thinning black hair, Duell smiled at Schnabel with an old-country sharpness.

"Not only do I hold a contract to buy Chauveron," he said. "I also hold contracts to buy the buildings on each side."

Schnabel was not about to take Duell's word for those claims. Getting the first whiff of an assemblage, Duell might be planning to tie up those very properties he claimed already to hold as soon as Schnabel was out the door. To check it out, Schnabel quietly asked the owner of the small apartment house at No. 145, sharing the east wall of Café Chauveron, if his building was for sale. The owner was an accountant named Morris Primoff.

"Gee," said Primoff, "I just made a deal."

Schnabel did not bother to ask if he had also signed a sales contract. Duell appeared to check out on two out of three claims. He probably did have three out of three. Schnabel was depressed. His careful research had shown no recent turnovers. Now, on his very first probe, he had bumped up against a smartster who, one step ahead, had carried out a mini-assemblage of his own.

Schnabel went back to the bank to see if it wanted him to dicker with Duell. It did. They parried through the summer.

"Who is this Lexman?" Duell kept asking. "Is it Uris, Fisher Brothers, maybe Tishman?"

"Manny," intoned Schnabel, "All you have to know is that my money is green."

His money was green, his pockets deep. On August 13, 1969, Schnabel and Duell sat down with their lawyers to sign a deal. Lexman was buying the purchase agreements that Duell had himself signed with the owners of the three buildings and was now "flipping." In standard fashion, months would pass between signing the contract and conveying the deed. The buyer would use this time to nail down his financing and search the title to be sure the seller actually owns the property that is being sold. Meanwhile, the seller can check out the credit of the buyer. In the Lexman account at the Citibank branch at Madison Avenue and 42nd Street, Duell found a balance of more than $2 million.

Schnabel was sure that Duell would clear a handsome profit upon flipping the three contracts. Just how handsome, he did not realize until they sat down together. Duell had bought the Primoff building for $1.25 million. He was selling it to Lexman for $2.28 million. What really startled Schnabel, however, was the date that Duell had signed with Primoff: July 25. That was a month after Primoff had said he'd "made a deal." He would be sorry now. By turning away Schnabel so quickly, he had cleared the way for Duell to make $1 million on a contract that Duell had held for exactly 19 days.

Across the table now, Duell was beaming. In front of Schnabel, he could see a Lexman check ending in many zeros.

"Manny" said Schnabel, "Just one thing. If you want me to take over these contracts, I need to know that you are going to stay off the block from this month on. I don't want you popping up on the other side with more contracts. I want this to be goodbye, Manny."

"Don't you worry, Don. I'll be off the block."

"And I want your partners, your cousins, and anyone else fronting for your interests to stay off the block, too.

"I promise."

"I believe you," said Schnabel. "As a token of your good faith, I'm sure you won't mind signing over to me a $600,000 mortgage on one of the buildings you own. Maybe that nice one at 530 Sixth Avenue. We'll put it in escrow. If you stay off the block for 18 months, it reverts to you."

Manny Duell blanched. He leaped up and shook his fists. He swore that he would never, ever do such a thing. But Schnabel could see that even as Duell was ranting, his eyes were fixed on the check with all the zeros. Schnabel waited. When Duell calmed down, the mortgage belonged to Lexman.

From the dates on the contract for the Chauveron parcel, Schnabel could see that Duell actually had signed that deal when he said he had. But the deal for the Blarney Stone property, like Primoff's, was contracted well after Duell said he had. Just the same, Schnabel felt that he must have earned that one. The seller had been the partnership of Sol Goldman and Alex DeLorenzo, the toughest dealers in town. Predictably, Duell had not cleared nearly as much on the resale of that contract as he had on Primoff's.

As the moment came for the signing over of the three contracts, Schnabel assumed they would be transferred to Lexman from Duell personally or from a company he set up to buy them. The Primoff property, for example, had been purchased by Duell's 1045 Fifth Avenue Corporation. But Duell put up his hand.

"1045 doesn't own that contract any more," he said. "It's owned by another company."

"What company, Manny?"

"Mitmas Corporation.

Duell shoved a paper across to Schnabel. It showed that the Primoff contract had indeed been passed from 1045 to Mitmas Corporation, a "Panamanian company with principal offices at 10 Splugen Strasse, Zurich, Switzerland."

"What is this, Manny?"

"What it says," answered Duell. "You asked me not to worry who Lexman is because your money is green. Well, don't worry who Mitmas is because my contracts are black and white."

Duell snapped his fingers toward the door. A small, neatly dressed, elderly man hurried in, head down."

"Where do I sign?" he asked in a thick European accent.

Duell pointed to the places. The small man signed his name in neat but cramped script, "Frank J. Offenbacher." Then, head still down, he hurried out.

"He's Swiss," said Duell, as if that explained everything.

Even the Lexman lawyers were slightly taken aback by this scene. But when Julien heard about it later, it made perfect sense to him. "I can understand why a man would register a corporation in Panama," he explained. "The tax laws are as easy as anywhere. But put a big wad of cash in a Panamanian bank?" Julien shook his head. "They could have a revolution and burn the banks. But if you pay your taxes in Panama and bank your money in Zurich—that's security."

Schnabel now had to move fast. The first title was to be conveyed to Lexman in six months. Then it would be recorded at the county clerk's office. Brokers who regularly monitor those title transfers, as Schnabel did himself, would see that action was beginning on the formerly dormant block. From the tax stamps affixed to the deed, they would also know what Lexman paid. In the interim, Schnabel would have to nail down as many parcels as he could. The bank agreed that the next beachhead should be established on Lexington Avenue. They would "come ashore" at a restaurant named Trefner's. Eva Trefner had run it for 20 years—a hard daily grind. Schnabel felt that she would be ready to give it up. She was. But she was also hesitant.

"If I go, what will happen to my people?" she asked, motioning to the scurrying waiters and busboys. "They have families to support."

"If you go," said Schnabel, "I'll promise we'll operate the place for at least a year with the same staff."

Reassured, Eva Trefner sold her restaurant. Before she left for Florida, she divided a portion of the proceeds among her most faithful employees. The checks were not tokens. They went as high as $25,000. Trefner's did not close up for 18 more months. Around the corner, Café Chauveron hung on for almost as long after Lexman bought out the lease for $300,000. Soon after, Roger Chauveron reopened in Fort Lauderdale.

The owner of the Blarney Stone chain, Tom Donahue, always took long leases for his bars. The lease on the one next to Chauveron was 22 years. Donahue was no stranger to assemblages. His Blarney Stone lease on the site of the future Exxon tower on Sixth Avenue had been bought out for big money a few years earlier. Julien felt that nobody in his office was quite right to tangle with Donahue. So he hired a canny broker named Joe O'Gara to negotiate. O'Gara worked out a quick, if expensive, buyout of the Blarney Stone lease.

With his beachheads secure on 53rd Street and on Lexington Avenue, Schnabel now targeted the 54th Street flank. It was lined mostly with townhouses, including the five owned by St. Peter's. There was also the much larger Medical Chambers, jointly owned by 37 doctors. Prosperous and secure, they would be hell to buy out. Luckily, their building was far enough back toward Third Avenue so that the bank did not absolutely need it. In fact, an alternate plan had already been drawn up to erect the bank tower around the Medical Chambers. Rather than tangle with the doctors now, Schnabel decided to go after the small townhouse next door at No. 136. It contained a Deli City downstairs and a graphics studio upstairs.

In a common arrangement, Deli City was leased by a restaurant packager who installed kitchen equipment and subleased the premises to an operator. Deli City's owner of record was Pirates Cove Enterprises. Not to be outdone in the naming arena, Schnabel bought them out as Hayades Realty Corporation, named for the supply ship he had served on as a naval officer.

Now it was autumn. The time had come for Schnabel to find out if St. Peter's could be induced to sell.

"All I can reveal about my client," he told Dr. Peterson, "is that it is listed on the NYSE, that it has assets above $500 million, and it is not, I believe, in a business objectionable to you, like liquor or war munitions."

Dr. Peterson was charming and shrewd, but terrestrial real estate was not his line. So the church hired its own real estate consultant, John White, president of James D. Landauer Associates. As its negotiator, White was made to understand that the church was committed to staying at the center of the city. Yet it also needed a better facility for Dr. Peterson's active ministry.

Was it possible for both bank and church to get what they wanted? White came up with the solution: Make the new office tower a condominium. On its plaza, sell the church back its own corner. It would get a deed to its space just as if it were a residential condo owner. If St. Peter's wanted to be "more human in skyscrapers," and if Lexman's client wanted a distinction shared by no other office tower in town, this was their mutual chance.

Remarkably, the church still was in the dark about the identity of its suitor. Then, one day in February 1970, Schnabel told Dr. Peterson that his client would like to meet him. The only condition was ongoing secrecy.

At 7:30 that evening, a dark green limousine pulled up in front of Dr. Peterson's door. The minister settled into the rear seat and the tall, dignified man already sitting there handed him a business card. It read, "Henry Muller, Senior Vice President, First National City Bank."

The limousine sped downtown. Muller ushered the minister into a private dining room at Delmonico's, a hoary restaurant in the financial district. Muller had picked this spot because at that hour Wall Street was emptied out and they would not be noticed. Muller explained that he had been overseeing Lexman's day-to-day assemblage moves. He hoped that if the project went through, the church and the bank would be more than the sum of their parts. The two men hit it off. As it happened, Henry Muller was a Lutheran himself.

That same February, St. Peter's signed a letter of intent to sell its church to Lexman for $9 million. It would get a new and bigger structure of its own design on the same corner. As least 66 percent of it was to be free standing. The projected cost of the new church was $5.5 million. With interest on the original $9 million, that would leave a hefty $4 million for St. Peter's expanding programs. All this only was possible through the condomium arrangement.

Besides not wanting to be tainted by a morally objectional purchaser, St. Peter's also was concerned that there be no rough handling of residential tenants who were being forced off the block. The bank was possibly even more sensitive to that issue. It had built a reputation as the most progressive big bank in town. In no way would it be sullied by the image of palsied old folks being booted out of their homes.

That problem was real. As on most busy midtown blocks, residential tenants on this block went unnoticed in the commercial crush. Many were poor and old, even odd, and they often lost out when the wrecker showed up to flatten their homes. Tenants who played the game flawlessly, on the other hand, could wave goodbye to their old home and head straight to the bank. Alan Bandler, longtime lawyer for Studley, was once told by another lawyer about two young women living in a walk-up apartment in an East 58th Street building which was to be demolished as part of the assemblage on which the Four Seasons Hotel would be built. The other lawyer had refused to represent the two women, one of whom was a typist at his office, because his law firm did not take contingency cases, in which payment only comes with a settlement.

Bandler agreed to represent the two women. Or, as he puts it, "I gave them common sense advice: They should not say that they refused to move, but just tell the developer that they needed to talk to their families and friends. I told them to hold off as long as they could. Ideally, they would be the last tenants in the building. Then, when they were all that was holding up clearance of the site, we'd negotiate." The two women followed Bandler's advice and when they vacated the building they received $1.25 million. "Compared to what an extended construction delay would have cost, that wasn't so much," says Bandler.

On the Citicorp site, residential tenants were relocated with possibly less unpleasantness than ever before in the city's history of site clearings. This success owed more to psychology than to payouts. Rather than send a terse notice to a pair of frail octogenarian sisters named Julia and Alyce Belora, for example, McArthur visited them to ask whether they had someplace to go.

"If we moved, it would only be to our sister's place in California," said Alyce.

McArthur nodded. He ordered the best moving service he could find to follow the sisters' packing instructions exactly. He sent them a pair of first class tickets to Los Angeles and a limousine to take them to the airport. The sisters loved it. They even left without asking for a cash buyout, and once they were settled in California, they sent McArthur a thank-you note.

A special challenge was presented by a single man who lived in a rooming house on 54th Street just off Third Avenue. He was paying $6.90 a week for a small room, linen service included. He was a devout member of the Church of the Living God. Following biblical example, he walked to the East River each evening to pray by the swiftly flowing waters.

"I'll never move," he told McArthur. "Not unless God tells me."

Lexman sent a $500 donation to the church in the man's name. God then told him to move.

It was not so easy to satisfy Thomas Howard, a middle-aged bachelor who had lived for 22 years in his town house at 150 East 54th Street.

"They'll carry me out of here in a pine box," he told McArthur.

Howard's health was poor. He had no dependents. He hardly ever left the house. When he did, he usually hired a limousine. Apparently, he was financially comfortable. Why should he sell? McArthur gently persisted. He often visited Howard as he lay in bed in his purple bedroom, the walls covered with old paintings, the floor thick with small asthmatic dogs. One evening, McArthur brought over slides from his vacation in Portugal. Multiple dogs could not keep Howard from being lonely.

"Come often, Charlie," he said, "as long as it's only social. Because I'm never going to sell."

Just in case he changed his mind, McArthur and Schnabel decided to try to buy out the lease of Howard's only commercial tenant, Irene Allen, proprietor of a dress boutique on the ground floor. Allen looked like a tough, wary bargainer. If they went to her directly, she might well scent the assemblage. How could they get her lease without tipping their hand? The brokers went to Julien for advice.

"I know an actress, very chic," said Julien. "We'll give her a role."

One morning at a slow hour for the boutique, the actress, leggy and elegant, accompanied by a Lexman lawyer playing her sugar daddy boyfriend, chatted up Irene Allen.

"I'm an actress," she said. "Right now, I'm between shows. My boyfriend loves my taste. Until the right role comes along, he's going to set me up with a boutique. I've always admired yours so much. We wonder if you'd sell us your complete stock and your lease."

"I do very well, thank you," said Irene Allen, looking over the couple cooly. "Why would I want to sell?"

"To make a lot of money," said the sugar daddy.

Irene Allen was tempted, but after several meetings, she mentioned casually that she had asked for and received a five-year lease extension from Howard. Her one-year lease was now six. Plainly, its buyout cost had risen steeply. The brokers were miffed. But Julien, thinking moves ahead, was delighted. Where they saw a blockage, he saw an opening.

If Irene Allen could get a lease extension out of Howard, maybe she could get other considerations. Julien had one in mind.

At their next meeting, the couple asked Irene Allen if she could deliver a right of first refusal clause to buy the town house. She came back the next week with the clause signed by Howard. That was a coup. Now if any speculator somehow charmed Howard, he or she could not buy the house unless Irene Allen (or whoever held her lease) turned it down first.

McArthur dickered with Howard, his attorney, and his accountant for months after Irene Allen sold them her lease for a tidy sum. He was still not selling. A year, then two, passed. Finally, Julien decided that the deal had to be made. An ultimatum would be delivered.

"Tom, we're going to draw up a contract," McArthur told Howard. "It'll be good for 48 hours. The space for the purchase price will be blank. Fill it in with the number that you think is right. We'll say yes or no in those 48 hours. If we say no, Tom, I promise you'll never be bothered by us again."

Howard inserted the figure $815,000 in the blank. The bank instructed Lexman to accept it. Howard moved to another brownstone on East 35th Street.

Two doors down from Howard, at No. 154, Schnabel got into a nasty imbroglio. Upstairs was The New Theater. Downstairs, marked only by a small brass plaque, was Oliver Coquelin's then trendy nightspot, Hippopotamus. Both leases required that the tenants get out within six months if the building were sold. Schnabel had no trouble buying the building and he was in no hurry to evict either tenant.

"You can stay for at least a year," he explained. "But you must agree to vacate on 30 days' notice when my client is ready to demolish."

"Fair enough," said the operators of the New Theater.

"Go to hell," said Olivier Coquelin.

It took a team of armed city marshalls and a court order to finally padlock Hippopotamus, which had continued to ignore its new landlord. The New Theater, which had been cooperative, continued to operate for another season.

The biggest prize on 54th Street was the Medical Chambers. But the prospect of making a deal with its 37 doctor-owners was unpromising. Given their tax brackets, the tax consequences of a cash offer were nasty. Trying an end run around that problem, Schnabel proposed to the doctors, late in 1969, a swap of their building for a bigger, nicer one renovated to their specifications. The doctors responded by firing their board of directors for even discussing the matter.

The next board was authorized to talk with Schnabel to the extent of rejecting an offer of $4 million for their building. On behalf of his client, Schnabel then offered to build a new Medical Chambers across the street. They could stay in their old quarters until it was ready. The doctors said no.

As the negotiations dragged into a third year, the doctors at last learned that their suitor was the bank. Despairing of ever making a deal with them, the bank suggested that they hire John White to represent them as well as St. Peter's. An easily bored man, White sat through many meetings with the doctors, trying not to look numb as they lectured him in detail on real estate strategy. White understood that they were not tempted to sell out for cash. Unlike the church, they would lose much of their windfall to taxes. Was there a way to make big money and also keep it?

Suddenly, the solution occurred to White. Citicorp was a stock company. So was the Medical Chambers. Why not merge them? In an exchange of shares, the doctors would get Citicorp shares that could not be taxed until sold. Even then, neither they they nor their children would pay more than the maximum capital gains tax, then 25 percent.

On a June day, three and a half years after the doctors' first adamant rejection, the SEC-registered merger of the 3000-share Medical Chambers and the 120-million share Citicorp was consummated. For each dollar of their stock, the doctors got Citicorp stock which was worth $30 by the time they had to vacate their building four months later.

Cantankerous as they were, the doctors were not the most difficult owners on the block. That honor went to two absentee children, heirs to an estate, who owned the shoddy building at the key corner of Lexington Avenue and 53rd Street. It was leased to a liquor store, an optometrist, and a Howard Johnson's counter service restaurant.

The children were represented by a lawyer named Gloria Del Vecchio. She soon became known to the two brokers simply as the "Executrix." In the fall of 1969, she explained to Schnabel that her wards had secured a steady income from the busy storefronts. Why should she sell on their behalf? To invest in stocks and bonds? The best of them would not yield a return as high as the commercial leases. Why indeed should Del Vecchio sell? The answer was obvious to both sides. She would sell as soon as the price was boosted high enough to give the children more income than they were currently getting.

Six months after bargaining began, Schnabel and the Executrix finally met to sign a purchase agreement in April 1970. She had been tough. The price per square foot was the highest that Lexman had yet paid on the block. But Schnabel took comfort in the thought that all three leases would soon expire, and he would be spared buying out any tenant for huge sums. However, at the signing, the Executrix had an unwelcome surprise.

"By the way, Don," she said. "Last fall, before I ever thought I'd be selling, the fellow from the liquor store and the optometrist asked me for a lease extension on their stores. I gave it to them."

"How long do the leases run now?" Scnhabel asked evenly.

"Twelve years."

"Oh." Schnabel was furious. If the lease extensions had been as long as two years, that would have been barely tolerable. But *12* years? He felt trapped. The assemblage was too far along to stop, the corner in question was a must-have, and the Executrix knew it.

Schnabel soon learned that it had not been the liquor store and optometrist owners who had asked for 12-year leases, as the Executrix had claimed. Instead, a totally new master lease had been awarded to a chunky, smiling man named Sam Salerno, operating as P.F.A. Enterprises Inc. Every few days, Salerno appeared in front of the building and stared benignly across the avenue at the current Citicorp headquarters. He also watched as, one by one, the wrecker's ball smashed down the other buildings on the block.

Salerno did not look like a man in a hurry to sell out his own lease. The bank was in no hurry, either. If it had no other choice, it would build around Sam Salerno.

On July 24, 1973, the bank announced it would build Citicorp Center, a 46-floor tower on 10-story stilts, designed by Hugh Stubbins. St. Peter's would occupy 45,000 square feet of the bank plaza exactly on its former footprint. Of shining aluminum and dark glass, the center would be topped off by a thrusting, south-facing plane at a 45-degree angle, meant to house solar energy collectors. Solar never worked out, but that slanted crown would impose itself on the skyline. Citicorp Center would be every bit as imposing as Chase Manhattan Plaza, maybe even more so. As one bank official then put it, the tower was to be "a priapic expression of Citibank's relentless hard-on for Chase."

One hot summer morning, the wreckers came to old St. Peter's Church. They yanked off the spires, smashed the finely detailed limestone walls, and shattered the graceful webbing that had held the stained glass. At noon, they sat on the rubble with their lunches and watched the girls. From his corner building, Sam Salerno watched them all.

In November, the dowdy Medical Chambers finally came down. All that remained was a small restaurant on Lexington Avenue whose lease would soon run out, and Sam Salerno's three tenants. He knew the bank wasn't bluffing when it threatened to build around him. But he also knew that both he and the bank would then be losers. As a street-wise fellow, Salerno must have been amazed that this mighty corporation, which owned the building, did not order a bulldozer to flatten it one night.

Late in 1973, the bank finally bought out Salerno's P.F.A. lease for $385,000. It had now paid $40 million for land and leases—until then, the highest ever for one block of city land. The only property not part of the assemblage was 880 Third Avenue, an 18-story office tower on the southeast corner of the block built in 1963. That property was impractical to buy out and, in any case, it was at the periphery of the assemblage. The bank would build around it.

Five and a half years after Schnabel and McArthur first walked the block, its 16 owners and dozens of tenants were gone. Up rose the tower and, tucked in its embrace, the church. Although New Yorkers are notoriously indifferent to retail arcades, especially underground, they embraced Citicorp's four floors of shops and eateries. The angular and austere reincarnation of St. Peter's pulsed with a new vitality. The church does not seem overshadowed by 59 floors of offices. You can look up from its interior directly at the sky—an impossibility in the old St. Peter's.

Except for 880 Third Avenue, all that had once been on the block—bars and restaurants, boutiques and medical offices, nightclub and theater, news dealer and town-houses—is forgotten. Then as now, the city of dreams and deals renews itself.

6 Last Day of the Downtown Office

If last year was your best year ever—
watch out for next year!

—Julien Studley

The offices of Studley's downtown Manhattan branch were on the 86th floor of One World Trade Center. They were airy, clean-lined, spacious and serene. The vistas of the harbor and beyond were vast. The walls were notable for Don Schnabel's collection of antique maps of Manhattan—some from so long ago that they still showed a wall on Wall Street. Twelve people worked in the downtown branch, which was managed by George Martin.

Martin had been Citicorp's key contact with Don Schnabel during the secret assemblage of the site for the bank's new tower in the early 1970s. The two men had stayed in touch. "In 1983," says Schnabel, "George told me the bank wanted to transfer him to Chicago, but he had already been posted in London and Toronto, and his family was tired of traveling. He was interested in joining us. We hadn't hired anybody with his corporate background, and he had no brokerage experience, but Julien felt the firm was ready for somebody like him."

It was also the right time, it seemed, to open a downtown office. Martin and Schnabel took space at 100 Wall Street in 1984, next at 199 Water Street, and then at 70 William Street. The final move, in February 2000, was to One World Trade Center. "It was a rainy Friday night, and a few of us made the move between 6 P.M. and 2 A.M.," says Barbara Kennish, a secretary in the office, who was then pregnant. "Don was neurotic about pregnancies," she says, "and he kept saying, 'Don't reach for this, don't lift that. . . .' "

On that fateful morning of September 11, 2001, the first to arrive was broker Robert Goodman, who commuted from Westchester County. As was his custom, he was at his desk by 7:30 A.M. A big man with a banker's starchy manner, Goodman is an elegant dancer who had performed a scintillating tango with Lois Zambo on the stage of a Buenos Aires nightclub during the 2001 Winter Trip.

Half an hour later, Jim Gartenberg arrived. For nine years, the slender, intense broker had been president of the local alumni association of the University of Michigan. He'd raised membership from a few dozen to about 400. Gartenberg had not been a college athlete, but nobody surpassed him as a fan of Michigan teams. Among the first words of Nicole, his two-year-old daughter, were, "Go Blue!"

Gartenberg, then an expectant father, was moving to another firm and, quite apart from the impending events of that morning, this was to be his last day at Studley. On the previous evening, he'd stayed late to clean out his desk and back up his files. Normally, he'd always be home in time to put Nicole to bed, but she was fast asleep by the time he arrived at his Upper East Side apartment carrying a calzone from a local pizzeria. Biting into it, he discovered mushrooms, a food that he hated. His wife, Jill, rewrapped the calzone and dashed out to the pizzeria to exchange it for one that was mushroom-free.

The third to arrive that morning, when the sky seemed purest blue, was 32-year-old Patricia Puma, a staff assistant. Puma, a mother of three young children, worked only the first two days of the week. Her best friend, Barbara Kennish, worked the other three. "Together, we made a whole," says Kennish, who also has three young children. For Puma, the arrangement was ideal. Her husband, Kevin, worked for the MTA and got a pay differential by working the 4 P.M. to midnight shift. Off on Sundays and Mondays, he was able to be there for their three children, ages 11, 7, and 3. Patricia's sister helped on Tuesdays, so that the Puma family had minimal need for babysitters.

The two families loved to vacation together. Kennish remembers the year they'd gone to the Catskill Game Farm where the kids "spent three days feeding disgusting food to the animals." Once, when a Studley family outing was slated for Key Largo, Florida, the Puma and Kennish families left a few days early for a fling at Disney World. "We weren't friends," says Kennish, "we were family." Both women were full of Brooklyn spunk and at the office, always lively on the telephone, but Kennish insists, "I was the mean one and Pat was the sweet one."

At 8:35 A.M., Goodman headed out to an appointment in midtown, leaving only Gartenberg and Puma in the office. Eleven minutes later, the first jetliner penetrated the North Tower, tearing a hole between about the 92nd and 96th floors. Debris and flaming jet fuel poured down, blowing in the glass of Studley's front door on the 86th floor and blocking it with a mountain of debris. A firewall leading to an emergency stairway also collapsed, sealing off the only other exit. A fireball had blitzed through the elevator shaft. On the opposite side of the 86th floor, workers in a less damaged Port Authority office would be able to walk down a stairway to safety. But the Studley office was sealed off to escape.

Don Schnabel was driving downtown with his wife Eileen, who also worked in lower Manhattan, when the first plane hit. He had no problem reaching Puma and Gartenberg by cell phone. Gartenberg wanted to know if he should break a window due to the smoke. Schnabel advised against it and suggested instead using George Martin's office because it had a fan which might help in blowing away smoke if the door was kept closed. He also suggested wetting the curtains.

Schnabel next called Julien at home. "Don told me to turn on the TV," says Julien, "and as I did, I saw the second plane hit." Nobody knew whether more attacks were coming, and Schnabel advised Julien to stay at home. But Julien dressed quickly and walked on Park Avenue to his office 11 blocks away. From his third-floor office windows, he saw two ministers in their robes standing on the steps of Saint Bartholomew's Church, offering comfort to passersby.

Margaret Luberda, the firm's human resources officer who had been on the job less than six months, had arrived at headquarters about 8:55, later than usual. "The receptionist said that we'd got a call from the downtown office and that they had this fire," says Luberda. "Neither of us had any idea of what had happened yet. Then somebody else called in and said a plane had hit the World Trade Center and I thought, God forbid, it must have been a little airplane and the pilot had a heart attack."

Amazingly, Luberda was able to call Gartenberg without any problem. Keeping the line open, she called 911. "I explained that I had two employees trapped on the 86th floor of Tower One," she says. "The operator patched me through to the fire department. These people sounded competent and said they were on the case. I switched back to Jim to tell him that help was on the way. I was trying to imagine what they were experiencing and figure out if there were any options. But there weren't." Puma, meanwhile, kept an open line to George Martin, who was at home.

As the smoke thickened, Gartenberg and Puma asked Luberda if they could "throw a chair through a window" to get fresh get air. Told that the windows were floor to ceiling, the 911 operator advised against it. They had water but were advised not to wet down their clothes.

In Chicago, Adam Goldman, Gartenberg's best friend since fourth grade, was watching the CNBC financial news at his office when the program was interrupted by the breaking news from the World Trade Center. The two men had been camp counselors together and best man at each other's wedding. Both were expecting a second child. Goldman dialed Gartenberg's number, as he did up to three times a day, and got through. Their conversation was recounted in a *Washington Post* story on September 15, 2001.

As a horrified Goldman watched the TV image of smoke rising from the first tower, he told his friend, "You want to get down, Jimmy." (People in the second tower were told to stay in their offices in the moments after the first tower was hit.)

"We can't get out of here," said Gartenberg.

"Stay calm," said Goldman.

"I can't stay calm with you, Adam. I'm afraid. Please get me out of here."

Gartenberg, using both the office phones and his cell phone, also heard from Andrew Rosen, a close friend since their freshman year at Michigan. Rosen was calling from his car in Englewood Cliffs, New Jersey. Bob Goodman's wife, meanwhile, had contacted a local TV station, which put Gartenberg on the air. In a calm voice, he told firemen where he and Puma could be located. He reassured the families of others who were trapped in the tower.

Puma talked several times to her husband, Kevin, whose late shift allowed him to be home for the kids. "She never told me about the smoke, because she didn't want to worry me," says Kevin. "And she didn't want me to tell her mom that she was trapped. The last time I talked to her, I told her I loved her, but I don't know if she heard me." When I saw the south tower go down, I knew the same thing was going to happen to the north tower. I shut off the TV when it happened and went up to our bedroom and cried."

Jill Gartenberg, a speech therapist, had arrived at her office on East 79th Street a few minutes after nine o'clock. She flicked on her answering machine. There was a brief, chilling message from her husband that she has never erased and that belies the calm that he showed on the air. In a hurried, trembling voice—"That's not the real Jimmy," said Jill, as she played the tape seven months later—Gartenberg tells his wife that there is a fire. "I don't know if I'm going to make it," he says. "I love you."

Jill called her mother-in-law, who lived nearby, and decided to go to her apartment. "I walked outside and from the sidewalk I looked downtown and saw black smoke billowing up," says Jill, who has always had a fear of death by fire. "I knew then that Jimmy wasn't getting out of there." At that moment, Jill screamed so loudly that people drew away from her. She screamed all the way to her mother-in-law's apartment.

The line was still open from the downtown office to Luberda in midtown. But, 30 minutes after the first plane had hit, the smoke was getting worse. "Can you breathe?" Luberda asked Puma.

"It's hard," answered Puma.

"Douse your jacket with water and breathe through it," said Luberda.

More debris was falling as the fire intensified from above. Gartenberg and Puma took cover under the reception desk to the left of the blocked and blown-out entrance doors. From there, they hoped to be able to call out to the firemen who were their only hope. Gartenberg and Puma had both been able to talk to their spouses before the lines finally went dead between 9:45 and 9:50. At 10:05, the south tower imploded. At 10:28, Armageddon replayed as the north tower collapsed. No remains or any sign of Puma or Gartenberg, or of the Studley office itself, would ever be found.

At noon, Barbara Kennish picked up her 11-year-old son, Matthew at school. He looked at her long and hard. "Mom, if you're here that means Patricia was at work this morning," Matthew said. He was crying in the car, so Patricia kept the radio off to keep from upsetting him more. When Kevin Puma picked up his son, Kiefer, he expected to wait until they were home to tell him what had happened to his mother. "But in order for us not to have to endure the ride home, I told him there," says Kevin. "We cried together."

For the next week, Patricia's two older children slept at Barbara's house. In Chicago, Adam Goldman held out hope that his best friend had survived for several days. One small nugget of hope was that Gartenberg's cell phone continued to ring when Goldman called it. If it had not been destroyed, perhaps its owner had not been destroyed. Goldman even located a survivor named Louis Lesce who, according to news reports, had walked down from the 86th floor of the north tower, passing fireman on the way up. But Lesce knew nothing of the people in the Studley office on the other side of the floor.

Many others held on to the hope that a loved one had survived and was in a hospital, as yet unidentified. Jill Gartenberg was not among them. After seeing the smoke rising from downtown, and perhaps even after hearing her husband's first desperate message, Jill Gartenberg harbored no illusions.

Julien Studley can be a highly emotional man. In the aftermath of September 11, however, he seemed strangely calm. "If I feel personally responsible for a bad situation," he explained, "I might get distraught. But I had no responsibility for the terrorist attacks." Moreover, the path of Julien's life has led to what he calls "a certain fatalism." He was born only nine years after the end of World War I in a country drenched with the blood of fallen soldiers. As he turned 13, he was caught up in the next world war. In this one, Jews like himself were marked for extermination by the Nazis. "In America, everyone thought that war would always happen somewhere else," says Julien. "Until September 11, most Americans had a certain innocence."

Julien had reached out quickly to offer what comfort he could to the Puma and Gartenberg families. "What I failed at first to realize," he admits, "was that people in the company who had not lost anyone in the attack were also traumatized and needed help. I'd done what I could for the families of the dead, but not for the living." So, in the first weeks after the attack, when air traffic had yet to return to normal and many feared to board an airplane, Julien began a schedule of visits to all 15 company offices where employees gathered with him to talk about their feelings in the aftermath of September 11.

On September 28, a packed memorial service was held at a Staten Island funeral home for Patricia Puma. Her tearful husband Kevin and 10-year-old Kiefer delivered eulogies for her, "or tried to," as one of the attendees said. Kennish continued to see the Puma family every week. She arranged for her son and Kiefer to be on the same little league team. Each of the Puma children carries a locket with a picture of their mother. "Kevin started a tradition of having the kids send up helium balloons with messages inside for Patricia," says Kennish. The first holidays after Puma's death were hardest for the surviving family, she says, starting with dressing up for Halloween in the costumes their mother had already bought. Kevin took the kids on their traditional pumpkin-picking expedition. At Christmas 2001 the kids still found their gifts under a tree, but for the first time ever, the outside of the Puma house was not decorated for the holiday.

Almost 1000 people attended the gregarious Gartenberg's memorial service held in an East Side synagogue. At the beginning of her eulogy, Jill held up the blue "game-day" Michigan shirt which she'd found hung in her husband's closet. "I used to hate it when he wore this jersey." she said, "I now treasure it." And she told how he would always dig into his pockets to give money to homeless people. "I, the nagging wife, would say, 'Jimmy, it's not like we have so much money that we can give it away like that.' He felt otherwise: In Jimmy's eyes we had more than they did and his gesture might give them hope."

Although Jill's eulogy was filled with positives about her husband, she did not neglect to appraise his killers: Those "responsible for destroying Jimmy's life and our world are evil, intolerant, vicious, judgmental, selfish, cruel, and jealous with no regard for human life. The irony—this is everything Jimmy was not—Jimmy genuinely believed in the best of people." Remembering their wedding vows, Jill said, "We knew it was 'til death do us part.' I just never imagined our parting would be after only 6½ years of marriage." Jill's final words were, "Go in love, go in peace, and GO BLUE!"

Patricia Puma's two older children will remember her, but her three year-old's memories will be spotty. The same is true for Nicole Gartenberg, who was two years and five months old on September 11. Watching a video in which Shirley Temple dances on her father's feet, Nicole piped up proudly, according to her mom, "I did that. I walked on my daddy's feet!" Everyone in the downtown office knew how thrilled Gartenberg was at the impending birth of his second child. Born in the spring of 2002, the daughter of James Michael was named Jamie Michelle.

September 11 will be remembered for the mass murder of nearly 2,700 individuals in the twin towers. A collateral sadness, easily overlooked, was the destruction of the hundreds of communities into which the dead and the rescued were grouped. Some were as large as Cantor Fitzgerald, almost a thousand strong, but many more were small, like Studley, close-knit in a way that larger firms could not be.

"I remember once," says Barbara Kennish, "that Jimmy Gartenberg bit into a chocolate bar without knowing it was filled with peanut butter. He hated peanut butter as much as he hated mushrooms. He stuck his head under the kitchen faucet like a dog lapping up water and we were all laughing. Don Schnabel came out of his office and said sternly, 'I didn't hear the recess bell. Why is everyone playing?' But when Don or George was ready to play, the recess bell always rung. We worked hard, but we had such a good time together."

7 Winter Trips, Summer Outings

We don't have a big ship to turn around, only our minds.

—Julien Studley

Customs officers did not open the black attaché case carried by broker Scott Pannick as he arrived in Egypt for the 14th Studley winter trip in January 1985. That was just as well. If they had peered in, Pannick would have been hard put to explain its diverse, even disquieting, contents.

Among the items within: two stuffed, yellow song birds in a small cage, a British passport in the name of Nancy Everleigh, a folding knife engraved "Jacque," its blade crusted with blood, a brass inlet valve labeled "Toxic Gas," one pill vial labeled "digitalis" and another printed in Japanese characters, and blueprints for a ship's ventilation system. There was an adoption certificate, a sales contract for a Sun Valley property, and a psychiatric report on a Studley director diagnosed as "a latently violent social hysteric." Also included were a novel called *An Indian Attachment,* a militant feminist magazine called *Off Our Backs,* and an issue of *National Geographic.* This last featured a story on fugu fish, prized by Japanese sushi enthusiasts who risk death if they accidentally come in contact with the fugu's poison.

Finally, and not least, the attaché case contained a snub-nosed revolver and 10 bullets. Upon close inspection, the gun would turn out to be a well-made fake. The 10 bullets were real.

Two days after arriving in Egypt, Pannick rose in the dining room of the luxury river steamer *Nile Dream,* where the Studley group of 50 was assembled for lunch. It was the beginning of a four-day cruise from Luxor to Aswan, centerpiece of this 1985 winter trip. Pannick, wearing a white suit and a false black mustache in the style of Inspector Hercule Poirot, made a shocking announcement: Peter Speier, head of Studley's suburban Washington office and vice chairman of the firm, had just been found dead in his stateroom. The cause of death was unknown but foul play was suspected.

It was a game, of course—a grown-up version of the kids' game "Clue." Pannick named it "Murder on the Nile." In the best tradition of Studley winter trips, the game was offbeat, intense, and designed to draw the brokers together even as they competed, maybe even cheated, to win a $1,000 prize. The challenge was to figure out how Speier had been murdered, who had done it, and what the motive was. Over four days, a web of clues would be woven, some helpful, others distracting. Pannick had a set of 40 handwritten cards just to keep track of the welter of clues. "Murder on the Nile" had been created with the help of Pannick's brother-in-law, a product and packaging designer in North Carolina.

Numerous persons had motives to kill Speier, as the clues scattered around the *Nile Dream* made clear. Was the culprit

Jacque Ducharme, who had received a letter from Arthur Anderson & Company informing him that Speier had been selected over him to undertake a lucrative project? Could it have been a broker whose embezzlement of $25,000 from Studley had been uncovered by Speier? What about Steve Goldstein, who had committed totally to a Sun Valley development deal that Speier threatened to quash? Another suspect was Pat Terry, a feminist who hated the "sexist-pig" Speier. So went the story line.

The real culprit was none of the above, the motive far from obvious. Of all the written solutions to the crime handed in by the final day of the cruise (they could be composed individually or by partners), only one, submitted by broker Jeff Shrago, correctly lined up seemingly unrelated clues and nailed the "who, how, and why" of Speier's murder.

Disregarding scads of misleading information, Shrago focused on an adoption document of an unnamed boy from 1958, then on the inscription scrawled in the novel, *An Indian Attachment.* It said, "Dear Son, Happy Birthday! Thought you might enjoy this after your foreign semester. Love, Mom." It was dated "12-29-77." Shrago also noticed that Nancy Everleigh's passport listed a son born in 1958 and had been stamped with a Delhi, India, visa in 1957. These and other clues led Shrago to identify Michael Geller, a broker born in 1958, as the secret son of Nancy Everleigh. But who was Geller's father?

Geller believed, according to Shrago's scenario, that the father he'd never known was Peter Speier, who had abandoned mother and son long ago. Speier had executed a "Last Will and Testament" on January 26, 1985, the first day of the cruise. It left the bulk of his estate to Nancy Everleigh.

By killing his own father, Shrago concluded, Geller intended that his mother would promptly receive the proceeds of Peter Speier's estate.

The weapon was not the gun, the knife, or (despite the pair of dead canaries found in Speier's stateroom) poison gas. The critical clue proved to be the copy of *National Geographic*, found in the *Nile Dream*'s engine room. According to the text of the article on fugu, the fish's poison is so toxic that an amount weighing less than half an aspirin could kill 30 adults. Shrago deduced that the pill vial labeled in Japanese characters contained fugu poison and that Geller had access to it. Other clues led him to a final deduction: Speier had expired shortly after signing and sealing his will. Licking the envelope, his tongue had touched a fatal coating of fugu poison.

Shrago won the $1,000 prize. For the company, the payoff was not so easy to measure, although no less real for that. Like all the winter trips, the Egyptian foray would seem to be, on the face of it, a reward for a year's work well done by the firm's top earners. Certainly, the trips are a morale builder. But, as Julien explains, "The morale factor is the least important element of the several things we're trying to achieve."

First comes the education factor. The longest waking hours aboard the *Nile Dream* were spent neither on sleuthing nor on dining, but in classes where brokers took turns being teachers and students. "The idea is to learn from each other," says Julien, "which can only happen when individuals open up to each other. The atmosphere back at the offices doesn't promote that. On the trip, it's time out and the brokers are willing to share secrets." At leisurely seminars, the year's major deals are explicated by the brokers who did them.

Clients often insist on secrecy, and even if they don't, the brokers tend to work behind closed doors. So this is often the first time that the word gets out on "what's gone down."

For astute brokers, information gleaned during Studley trips can unexpectedly come in handy. Michael Colacino, for example, took notes on a trip during which Art Greenberg of the Washington office discussed the intricacies of synthetic leases. A synthetic lease allows assets to be removed from a company's balance sheet to a single-purpose entity created for that purpose. Greenberg, an accountant before he became a broker, had once designed synthetic leases for aircraft owners. Although he has explored using them with client firms, Greenberg has yet to do a synthetic lease at Studley.

Several years after hearing Greenberg's discussion, Colacino was in the early stages of studying ways that Time Warner could finance its new corporate headquarters and studios at Time Warner Center on Columbus Circle. Time Warner's management broached the possibility of a synthetic lease. "Bingo! I thought back to one of our whacky winter trips and Artie's presentation," says Colacino. Time Warner, with Studley as consultant, went on to finance its presence at Time Warner Center with a $1 billion synthetic lease. Since the collapse of Enron, synthetic leases, along with other off–balance sheet devices, have come under fire. Accounting standards for synthetic leases are being modified. Greenberg compares synthetic leases to a car: "It's a dangerous vehicle. You need to be careful how you use it."

In the arena of business getting, brokers are competitive beasts. But the firm is not the arena, and colleagues are not supposed to be at each other's throats. "We try to make the brokers understand the spirit of competition," says Julien. "If somebody else among them is very strong, very competitive, that person can be a resource as well as a competitor. In the view of the outside world, that person's achievement is also their achievement because few outsiders will know the name of the individual broker. They perceive only that the deal was done by Studley. On the trip, that achievement in the marketplace becomes a learning experience."

When the brokers are let loose to compete among themselves on the winter trips, there is method to the mayhem. In Oaxaca, Mexico, in 1996, the group was divided into teams for a scavenger hunt. Each team was given a list of items to locate, ranging from a pound of pinto beans to a tire repair kit. Racing around the crowded city, the teams were as inventive in hindering their competitors as in checking off their shopping lists. One team even hired a taxi to block a narrow road out of the central marketplace—after it had made its own exit.

Judging the winning effort wasn't easy. Both speed and thoroughness counted. Although one team was the fastest to complete its tasks, another that was only slightly slower had managed to be more precise in bringing back the goods. Picking the winner, according to Julien (who was not a judge), required a "Solomonic judgment." "The debate was heated," says Julien. "The judges called it a tie because they decided that it was equally important to be the fastest and to be the most completely accurate at a slightly slower speed."

The slant toward group adventure became the bedrock concept of the Studley winter trips, separating them from standard corporate getaways to posh and placid golf and beach resorts. In the freed-up atmosphere of the winter trip, it's not only the deals that get discussed. "Our brokers say this is the only place that they can freely discuss their income," says Julien. "They also air out family issues that would not come up back at the office"

On the *Nile Dream*, even cabin assignments were designed to strengthen ties within the firm. Senior brokers shared a cabin with juniors, or at the very least, brokers at similar levels were assigned to room with brokers from another city. Brokers who had a dispute in the previous year would, like it or not, end up together.

"We recognized early on that if we were to going to have offices in different cities," says Don Schnabel, "we'd generate cross business. Suppose I have a client in New York who needs 8,000 square feet of space in Los Angeles. I need to be able to call a broker there who I may know primarily from winter trips and to whom I am comfortable saying, 'Look, it's important to me to maintain the relationship with this client, so do this for me even though it's a small thing.'" Schnabel emphasizes that trusting a colleague is not enough. Personality is equally important. "Let's say my client is kind of uptight," explains Schnabel. "It won't help to put her in touch with a broker whose style is laid back. I'm going to find her somebody who is also uptight. Interacting with people on the trips, you can gauge personalities."

With Julien's concept of firm as family, it might have seemed natural to pack off core members on an annual vacation. But the winter trips were only inaugurated once Julien decided to create an alternative to the annual dinner of the Real Estate Board of New York (REBNY). That affair was invariably held on the last Thursday in January at the Waldorf Astoria or the New York Hilton. Men dressed formally and the menu stuck close to roast beef, potatoes, and cherries jubilee. Studley, although smaller than many other member firms, always purchased a table right through the 1960s. After the dinner, the brokers walked over to Julien's apartment on East 60th Street and played poker.

On the afternoon before the REBNY dinner in 1968, the firm departed from habit by holding a general meeting in a rented conference room at the Manufacturer's Hanover Bank on Fifth Avenue. "We saw each other every day, but we didn't talk to each other," says Schnabel. "Everyone scurried into his little cubby hole. That's why we needed to meet outside the office." That predinner meeting set Julien to thinking: Why not leave the city during the week of the next REBNY dinner and convene a Studley-only "shadow" dinner far away?

Then a bachelor, Julien traveled frequently for pleasure. Offbeat, yet eye-opening destinations were his norm. One that had impressed him was Cartegena, on the coast of Colombia. Founded in 1533 as a Carribean port from which the Spanish conquistadors shipped their booty of gold and precious stones back home, Cartagena remained a picturesque city still touched by colonial formality and charm. If it was an unlikely destination for a corporate getaway, so much the better.

The risk-tinged sense of adventure that would color the Studley trips came early and unplanned. Looking out the window of the Colombian national airliner taking them south in the night, Julien noticed flames shooting from one engine followed by an announcement from the cockpit that the engine had been shut down but that it was too late to turn back. The plane landed safely in the provincial capital of Baranquilla. It was a nerve-twisting way to learn that difficult moments are remembered more than formulaic luxuries. As the group gratefully deplaned on a steamy tarmac in the summer heat, it was obvious that not everyone knew in which hemisphere Colombia was located. Gerald Freeman, the firm's press agent, was still wearing a full-length raccoon coat.

On the trip's final evening, all present dressed formally for the first Studley annual "commitment dinner," held at a Colombian naval officers' club. Julien asked each broker to stand up and announce his commission goal for the new year. In later years, brokers' goals were tracked by office managers before the winter trip. Back then, commitments were a critical tool. "Who had a better sense for how we would do in the coming year than the brokers?" asks Julien. "Looking back, we found that the sum of the brokers' expectations were always within 5 percent of the firm's total revenues for that year." Each broker still "commits" at the final dinner of each winter trip, but the act is now more ritual than tool.

Portugal was the destination of the second winter trip, planned by Charles MacArthur, Schnabel's partner in the Citicorp assemblage. The commitment dinner was held at Sintra, a royal castle near Lisbon. The brokers arrived in a procession of classic cars, with Julien leading the way in an open Rolls Royce. Julien's travel enthusiasms were again reflected in the choice of Chichicastenango, Guatemala, as the destination of the third winter trip in 1973. A vibrant Indian market town in the highlands, Chichicastenango was possibly even less familiar to the brokers than Cartagena had been. A bus ride over bad roads brought the group from the capital of Guatemala City.

The local Indian culture blended Christian and pre-Columbian traditions, especially in its cathedral. In the chill hour of dawn, the staff of the city's only real hotel entered each room to light, in lieu of central heating, a wood fire. All remember what should have been an uneventful crossing of seven-mile-wide Lake Atitlán, a high and deep mountain lake of volcanic origin. At the midway point, one broker suddenly asked, "How do you say 'pump' in Spanish?" The boat was taking on water and only energetic baling kept it from sinking before reaching the far shore.

Cartagena and Chichicastengo were off the beaten track. But not as far off as Yelapa, a Mexican hideaway that was the destination of the 1983 winter trip. "Mexico didn't even know it had Yelapa," insists David Raspler. Although on the mainland, Yelapa was only accessible via a two hour trip on an oceangoing ferry from Puerto Vallarta. The main clientele of Yelapa was "heavy-duty hash smokers," observed Howard Sadowsky, who had scouted out the place on a planning mission.

The dropped-out atmosphere of the Yelapa hotel—really a collection of thatched huts—was established at the open-air check-in desk, which the brokers noted had a single telephone with several feet of cord plugged into . . . nothing. Checking into his hut, Raspler discovered that his bed "was still being built." Netting covered each bed to protect against scorpions as well as insects. Guests were warned to check inside their shoes before putting them on, since scorpions like to crawl into warm damp places. Raspler went to bed "with my collar up and my jeans tucked into my socks." Rather than think about a scorpion in bed, a few brokers fled to the beach where they stayed up all night around a bonfire—only to be visited by Mexican boys who displayed oversized "pet" tarantulas. Uncharmed by the vicissitudes of Yelapa, two women brokers cut short their trip and returned to civilization.

Even Julien, a hardened tropical traveler, did not escape fear of scorpions. That first night in Yelapa, he awoke in a panic as something thudded onto his chest. He was sure it was alive and venomous until, when it didn't attack, he gingerly put his hand on it in the dark. It was his shoe. In what had seemed like a clever move, Julien had hung his shoes upside down on the bed posts. One had fallen on him. The only lights in the rooms were, according to Raspler, "yartzeit [memorial] candles."

The upside of Yelapa, says Howard Sadowsky, defending his choice, was that it was like "a Polynesian fantasy island—no jet skis, just rowboats, horses waiting to be ridden, fresh seafood and grilled vegetables in the only restaurant on the beach, and kids who would come around selling homemade banana pie." There was even an old woman who would "give you a shot" in case of a scorpion bite. Countering the opulent productions of prior years, commitment night in Yelapa was held around a beach bonfire. "Somebody had brought a guitar," says Sadowsky, "and that was it for props."

That wasn't totally "it." A master of contrast, Sadowsky had preceded the three-day Yelapa interlude with three-days of high-end dining and museum hopping in Mexico City. "I couldn't just take the guys to the beach," says Sadowsky. "First I had to enliven them."

Planning a northern California winter trip five years later, Sadowsky reversed the segments, this time upshifting from primitive to privileged. That 1989 trip began with an overnight at a Boy Scout camp high in the rugged mountains of Mendocino County. By day, there was horseback riding and hiking. By night, there was only the howling of a damp and frigid wind of a Pacific storm. Sadowsky had trucked in space heaters, but they short-circuited the camp's meager power supply. That night, 65 brokers, whose incomes many times exceeded the national average, shivered the night away. Arriving the next day at Meadowbrook Lodge, a resort in the temperate Napa Valley, they thawed out in style. Sixty-five masseuses, some brought in from as far away as San Francisco, were waiting to knead out each "camper's" weary muscles. The next morning, the group donned traditional whites to play croquet in the style of the British upper crust on the lawn of the lodge.

Studley's winter trip itineraries are no stranger to luxury hotels, but the bias is against them. "The crazy trips are the memorable ones, forget the comfortable ones where people complain about the sauce at dinner," says David Raspler. Even those trips can suddenly veer into a different mode. During the 1981 trip to Venice, Julien grew tired of hearing gripes from brokers who didn't like the view—or lack of it—from their rooms at the Danieli, the city's best hotel. It was time to liven things up. During a dinner at a restaurant hidden away on the far side of the island, Julien announced a contest to see who, at the end of dinner, could be the first to find his or her way back to the Danieli through the labyrinthian streets of Venice. Contestants could go solo or in teams. The winner would collect $2,000.

Fair play was out of the question. One female broker, entered the kitchen and tried to "romance" the chef into taking her back to the Danieli. Howard Sadowsky feigned cramps and called for a water ambulance. One team blocked off a key exit street. "The mentality of the group," says Sadowsky, "is such that Julien could have offered a lollipop instead of $2,000 and they still would have competed full blast."

Nothing is left to chance during the winter trips. "The dessert you'll eat at dinner on day 4 was already sampled months earlier by a trip planner," says Peter Speier, a veteran of the process. Still, things go wrong—sometimes woefully so. During the 1994 Chilean trip, the group was scheduled to go by boat from the harbor of Puerto Montt, on the untamed Patagonian coast, to a resort on a glacial island. Tides rush fiercely through Puerto Montt's narrow outlet to the sea. Departure was set for noon, when the ship could take advantage of the outgoing current. But one broker had missed the bus and the group wanted to wait for him. The captain was anxious. Once the tide turned, he warned, the ride would not be pleasant. That turned out to be an understatement.

The day was grey and windy when the boat finally headed out fighting the current. As waves slammed in, the boat barely made headway. The brokers held tightly to their benches and many became seasick. One, hanging over the rail, earnestly pleaded for anyone with a pistol to put him out of his misery. What should have been a 2 hour trip took 12 hours. Group hardships such as scorpion alerts and an unheated Boy Scout camp in winter tend to be recalled with fondness in later years. Not so the boat ride from Puerto Montt.

Winter trips are normally private events, but the 1993 trip to Brazil had a notorious aftermath. In the first phase, the group checked into a "tree hotel" in the Amazonian jungle. A soccer game was arranged with the local Indians. "Their players were short and fast, and there was no way to get around them," says Julien. "Maybe we'd have done better if we'd taken off our clothes like them." To the victors, the Studley team left their soccer equipment. By night, the brokers ventured into the river in dugout canoes to hunt for crocodiles, located by the glow of their eyes caught in the beam of flashlights. Kurt Handschumacher remembers watching a monkey sitting in a tree at the tree hotel with a purloined copy of a newspaper. The animal kept turning the pages around and around with its paws, as if looking for the secret to reading the news. From time to time, it swigged from a Coke can clasped by its tail.

Near the end of the trip, the brokers stayed in a riverfront hotel in Manaus, a sprawling city in the jungle heartland. The commitment dinner was to be held on a beach on the far side of the mile-wide Rio Negro. First timers were paraded blindfolded in grass skirts out of the hotel lobby to a waiting boat. A *National Geographic* photographer also staying at the hotel, assigned to do a picture essay on the Amazon basin, noticed the unusual goings-on and wangled an invitation to come along for the ride.

The captain delayed departure until a thunderstorm passed by. The newcomers remained blindfolded. Showers continued during the 30-minute trip in the open boat and drenched them. On the other side, they were daubed with "war paint," adorned with feathers, and then tied to partly-submerged trees in the knee-deep, dank water of the Rio Negro. "By then, these guys were a little chilled and not feeling so great," says Handschumacher. They remained in the river for only a few minutes. But that was long enough for the photographer, Alex Webb, to get his shots. One of them was selected to be included in the *National Geographic* issue of February, 1995. It showed five nearly naked brokers, hands tied from behind and heads bowed. They seemed to be prototypes for the future TV show, "Survivor."

Learning of the magazine's intention to print the photo, Julien reacted unhappily. "I told them it was unfair to us," he says. "The photographer came along as our guest. He hadn't told us that he was on assignment. And now they wanted to publish this photo without explaining the context. It looked like Studley was torturing its people."

Julien persuaded *National Geographic* not to mention the firm's name in the caption. The "victims" were identified only as New York–based real estate brokers. The striking photo was republished in Webb's book, *Amazon: From the Floodplains to the Clouds,* and in *Harper's* magazine. The only identifiable broker in the photo, Michael Colacino of the midtown Manhattan office, keeps a large print of Webb's photo on his office wall. Colacino may be the only Harvard man ever to be mistaken for a vanquished jungle warrior.

Defending the firm's induction ceremony in a *Dow Jones News Service* interview in 1998, Jacque Ducharme pointed out that newcomers weren't the only ones to undergo rugged treatment. During the 1996 winter trip to Israel, he recalled, the brokers were sent out into the Negev desert wearing Arab robes and kaffiyehs. "All I could think about was what the heck the Israeli army is going to make of this," said Ducharme. "We thought the bombs would fall on us any minute."

Along with their common experiences, winter trip veterans speak of intense personal memories. For Ducharme, an admirer of the classical world, it was the sight of a "fabulous Greek temple, made of volcanic stone and in perfect shape," in Agrigento, Sicily. For Mike Solomon, it was seeing "beautiful Indian women in Chichicastenango carrying jugs on their heads, putting me in touch with a people more gentle than us." For Paul Schweitzer, it was watching snow beginning to fall outside the Moulin de Mougin, a fabled restaurant in Provence, during his first three-star dinner in 1986. For Handschumacher, it was leaning on the rail of the *Nile Dream*, watching peasants carrying on their river-oriented life exactly as their ancestors had done for millennia. George Martin remembers the emotion he felt standing in the Garden of Gethsemane, "a place my mother had told me about since I was three or four years old."

Howard Sadowsky, like Schweitzer, still mentally savors that dinner at Moulin de Mougin. It's not the falling snow that most enchanted him, but the knockout first course of "truffle stuffed zucchini blossom in a veal essence." His personal high point, however, came on the eve of Mardi Gras in Rio de Janiero. A class in samba dancing was held in a suburban "poor man's bull ring."

"Kids started to play on home-made instruments," says Sadowsky, "Suddenly an 80-year-old, toothless old woman jumped up and started dancing to this unbelievable beat. I don't care how old or how uptight you are, you're dancing. It was one of the great moments of my life."

The winter trips created a sense of a corporate family. But the blood family was left behind. Julien rectified that situation in the 1970s by starting an annual summer outing to which spouses and children were invited. The first one was held on a Saturday in August at a Long Island estate belonging to the parents of Richard Zausner, then a Studley broker. The few children attending each received a gift from David Raspler, acting as a summer Santa Claus. By the turn of the century, the summer outings had become weekend-long events and grown so large—more than 800 attendees—that few hotels could accommodate them. In 2000 and 2001, the summer outing was held at the Loews Miami Beach, a megahotel with off-season availability. The bill for these outings was nearly $1 million. "If we were a publicly owned company," says Julien, "we could have a hard time convincing shareholders that the money is well spent."

For the kids, the high point of the summer outings was always Raspler's routine as gift giver. He knew how to work a young crowd, first making sure that he could put a name to each face and know a few facts about each child. Then he might say:

> Now there's a little girl from California,
> Her name begins with the letter A,
> She has a baby sister,
> And she just learned to swim...

Well before Raspler had spun out his verse, the child in question would be a bundle of gesticulating, tantalized excitement. But he took no notice until he was ready. "I'd make them crazy," he says. At the 1999 summer outing, held in Sun Valley, Utah, just before his retirement, it took Raspler three hours to present gifts to almost 200 children.

Raspler had been the Danny Kaye of winter trips, too. George Martin remembers how, after the umpteenth ambitious course at that memorable dinner at Moulin de Mougin, Raspler waved his white linen napkin from his fork to signify that his stomach had surrendered—a brave gesture in a temple of haute cuisine.

On January 25, 1988, the birthday of Robert Burns, Scotland's national poet, Raspler put on his most stirring performance. The 60 brokers celebrated the occasion with a dinner at the eighteenth century Hopetoun House, an imposing Scottish estate now the home of the Marquess of Lithlingow. The group wore traditional Scottish garb, delivered from a theatrical costume renter in London. Seamstresses were on hand to adjust the ladies' long tartan skirts and blouses with white sashes. George Martin was complimented by Captain Fox, the estate manager, on the authenticity of the tartans. "The way you Americans usually dress up," chided Captain Fox, "you look like Idi Amin's honor guard."

An actor recited Burns's poem, "Ode to the Haggis," a traditional dish in which a sheep's stomach is stuffed with offal, porridge, and lard. Then came the ceremonial "slaying of the haggis," in which a knife is plunged into the sheep's stomach. A fife and drum corps played. Little haggis but much Scotch was consumed.

Then the boisterous brokers piled into two buses to return to their hotel in Edinburgh. The night was cold, rainy, and murky. On the way out of the enormous property, along the Royal Drive, named after the kings and queens who had traversed it, the second bus mistakenly arrived at a gate that was too narrow to pass. When the driver tried to back up, the bus slid off the road and became mired in deep mud. Thirty men in kilts could not dislodge it. With the first bus long gone, the only thing to do was hike back to Hopetoun House and ask for shelter until help could be summoned.

They could not arrive at the door of their hosts, David Raspler decided, bedraggled, muddied, and defeated. "We'd do this like proper English brigadiers," he says. Raspler lined up the brokers in a double column. As they approached the grand entrance of Hopetoun House, the proprietors must have heard them coming, because they were standing in the open doorway. "I had our guys marching along and swinging their arms as only the English can," says Raspler. As they filed past the Marquess and Marquessa of Lithlingow, Raspler called out, "Eyes right," and they whistled the Colonel Bogie March, just as the Brits had done in a famous scene from the 1957 movie, "Bridge Over the River Quai."

As Studley has grown, it has inevitably become more corporate, even hiring a human resources manager in 2001. The winter trip entourage now includes guest speakers, such as a South American human rights advocate in 2000 and a member of Bill Clinton's White House staff in 2001. With Raspler's retirement, old-timers feel that the winter trips have lost their freewheeling spirit. But it's far from extinct, if my own experience as a guest on a pair of recent winter trips is any guide. I returned with my own indelible memories—including the classic event that went awry.

It started out, typically, with high promise. Debarking at the small airport in Baroloche in northern Patagonia during the 2001 winter trip, we discovered not the usual charter buses waiting for us but a caravan of Land Rovers. Battered and dusty, they looked like they'd been recycled from unwashed service on the Serengeti veldt.

Six to a vehicle, we were soon ricocheting up a merciless dirt road into the Andean foothills. High up on a sheer-walled peak was the abode of South American condors, the world's largest bird. Now I understood why we had each been given a pair of binoculars at the beginning of the trip. We were going condor watching.

The condors lived in caves on that sheer peak. They could simply fall out of their homes and be instantly airborne, rather than having to lift their great weight from earth. To induce them to come out for our benefit, two freshly slaughtered sheep carcasses had been placed on an escarpment near our viewing point. Since the condors, the 747s of the aviary world, could carry off a sheep, the carcasses had been staked down. A broker in my Land Rover cracked, "What line on the budget do we use for two slaughtered sheep?"

A chill and whistling wind mocked this supposedly summer day. Our guide explained that the condors, wiser than us, preferred to stay snug in their caves until better weather came. With binoculars, I was able to make out the profile of what appeared to be a condor in a cave, seemingly staring out. Watching us humans was the better part of the deal.

Bumping down the mountain, there wasn't much chitchat about condors. But the conversation in our Land Rover roamed effortlessly from one broker's scary experience with a burning Volvo station wagon back in Chicago to just how much relaxation is provided by a Tokyo masseuse. Spirited verbal abuse was heaped on Peter Speier and Paul Schweitzer for having planned this folly. Yes, it was a bonding experience—perhaps even more so than if the condors had cooperated. It was a reminder that Jacque Durcharme calls Studley "the Saint Jude of brokerage firms," referring to the patron saint of lost causes.

A quite different version of the unexpected had occurred, a year earlier, in Barcelona. The third morning's schedule of the winter trip had simply listed "games." I assumed that meant playing volleyball on the beach in front of our hotel. Trip organizers Peter Speier and Lois Zambo had a grander vision. Buses took us to the 95,000-seat stadium built for the 1990 Summer Olympics.

In the parking lot, event organizers divided the group into eight teams of 10 persons each. Caps and headbands in team colors were handed out along with a banner on a pole for each captain. Marching into the vast, empty stadium, with Julien at the head carrying an Olympic torch, we retraced the decade-old footsteps of the athletes. The sound system erupted with the cacophonous anthem of the 1990 Summer Olympics, as performed by Freddie Mercury and Monserrat Caballé.

The oval field had been readied for a half dozen events including sprints, archery, tug-of-war, basketball, and a wheelbarrow race. Here, where the fleetest athletes had struggled for glory, I hesitated to put down my own pair of sluggish feet. But only for an instant, because we were swiftly lined up by trainers who led us in calisthenics. Our warm-up concluded with a lap around the track as the stadium reverberated with the theme from *Chariots of Fire,* the 1981 film that opens with young British runners training on the beach for the 1924 Paris Olympics. With the surge of melody, my step seemed suddenly lighter, even weightless, and I felt as if I could lope on effortlessly and always.

Brokers do as they must to reach the finish line of a deal. Maybe even make their own rules. I know I did, competing blindfolded in the hurly-burly of the wheelbarrow race. By wiggling my nose and tilting my head up, I was able to see a bit of the track below my blindfold as I pushed my passenger. That kept me in my lane and moving efficiently. In order to make it seem as if I really couldn't see, I crashed into anyone in my way. If they tipped over, so much the better. In the "senior" 100-yard dash, I'm convinced that Ducharme, president-elect of the firm and in the lane to my right, jumped out ahead of the gun. Otherwise, in no way could he have beaten me by a stride. Absolutely no way.

The final event of the Studley Winter Olympics was played out at eight tables on the field. They were stacked with art supplies and sundry odd objects: wire, foam blocks, beads, colored tapes, paints, and sculpting clay. This competition was to team-build the best multimedia work of art within 15 minutes. In that interval, brokers reverted to kindergartners. The winner was determined by popular vote (it was forbidden to vote for one's own creation). In a departure from the athletic events, nobody seemed to care about victory in the art realm.

That evening, a dressy dinner was held at one of the extraordinary houses in Barcelona designed by Antonio Gaudi. After the cocktail hour, we drifted into the dining room. In lieu of the usual floral centerpieces on the tables were the sculptures created earlier in the day. Amid the formal silver and porcelain settings in this fantasy house, they took on the look of real, wild art. Even Gaudi might have approved.

I no longer remember that evening's menu, or anything about my team's sculpture. But I have not forgotten the malicious pleasure of crashing into others in the wheelbarrow race while peeking from under my blindfold. Nor have I forgotten seeing Jacque Ducharme's heels in the 100-yard dash. Most vividly, I remember how the big theme from *Chariots of Fire* took the weight out of my feet on the cinder track. Undeservedly, I felt touched by Olympic glory. And by the inventiveness of Studley winter trips.

Just one month after selling his shares in Studley, Julien went on the 2003 winter trip to Austria, for the first time not as leader but as a guest of new chairman Mitch Steir. The 2004 winter trip was planned as a Carribean cruise aboard a ship leaving from San Juan, Puerto Rico. Julien was again invited to be a guest, but this time with some embarrassment. Space being extremely tight on the cruise ship, he could not be assured a comfortable cabin of his own. Julien had a better solution. "I called my brother George," he says. "He has a home in Sag Harbor on Long Island, where he knows boating people. He put me in touch with a yacht broker. In 15 minutes, I was able to charter a 90-foot yacht docked in Virgin Gorda in the British Virgin Islands, where the Studley cruise was headed. The first mate doubled as an excellent chef. I invited my assistant, Marion Kennedy, to come along with her boyfriend."

The sleek white yacht, called the *MJ*, sailed alongside the cruise ship for two days. The symbolism could not be missed. Julien had cast off all lines to the ship he had built. A new captain was steering it. Yet his presence was still felt.

8 Newseum Goes to Washington

My idea of a grand corporate plan is listening to the needs of tenants. And my own needs.

—Julien Studley

Lois Zambo tells a story of how she did a long-ago deal that shows why a broker working at top form needs equal parts of determination and imagination if the deal is to get done. The bigger the deal, the larger the parts, as Zambo would prove 20 years later, when she carried off one of the grandest deals in the annals of commercial real estate brokerage. Zambo's actions also demonstrate that in order to get behind a client, sometimes a broker must get out in front of him or her—especially when she happens to be barely five feet tall.

This saga began in 1980 with a query from a partner at a law firm represented by Zambo in Studley's Washington office. "He had a client who wanted to know if it was unusual for a real estate broker to demand a guaranteed fee no matter if the deal was done or not," says Zambo. "When I learned that this client was *USA Today* and that it needed 60,000 square feet of space, I said, 'I want to talk to these people.'"

Zambo was raised as an Air Force brat whose first career was as a dental technician. It lasted six years and, she says, "I hated every minute of it." In 1975, she was hired as a receptionist and typist by Steve Goldstein, head of Studley's Washington office. Her starting salary of $6,000 was commensurate with her typing skills. "Steve thought there was something wrong because I used so many white-out ribbons on my IBM Selectric," she says. Leaving her typewriter behind, Zambo quickly moved up to brokerage, assigned to work with the late Edward Giesinger. The pair did a presentation for *USA Today,* which was then gearing up for its launch as a national newspaper. "We wowed them," Zambo says.

USA Today was seeking a substantial chunk of office space in an extremely tight commercial market in Washington, D.C. Moreover, if the newspaper proved successful, it would need to expand from 60,000 square feet to as much as 200,000 square feet. At the time, that kind of space with an expansion option was difficult to come by in the city. "The landlords were really feeling their oats," says Zambo. "They'd even try to pass through their debt costs to the tenant."

Zambo identified an opportunity just across the Potomac River in Rosslyn, Virginia. There, a 31-story office tower, slated to be the tallest building in the heavily horizontal Washington area, was under construction. The developer, Westfield Realty, had lured the Federal Communications Commission from Washington as prime tenant. But when mayor Marion Barry realized that the FCC was planning to slip away to Virginia, he mustered congressional support to stop the deal. Alarms were sounded that the new office tower would not only be a giant sore thumb sticking up over the low-slung Washington skyline, but it might also pose a hazard to flights approaching nearby National Airport. The protests did not stop the tower from being built, but they did force the FCC to back off from executing its lease. That freed up most of the space in Westfield's tower.

Zambo called Jimmy Thomas, chief financial officer of Gannett, the parent company of *USA Today*, and told him about the Rosslyn opportunity. *USA Today* could have its 60,000 square feet, along with expansion rights, at about half the rental rate downtown.

"The nation's newspaper can't be in Virginia," answered Thomas, relaying the dictum of Al Neuharth, founding editor of *USA Today*. "It has to be in the capital." And he hung up. After resurveying the market, Zambo called Thomas again. She was certain that the Rosslyn tower was the best solution for the *USA Today*. Thomas's answer was still no. It was the point where a less impassioned broker would have given up. But the more Zambo looked elsewhere, the surer she was that the Westfield tower was the right choice.

She dialed Thomas's number a third time.

"If you call me one more time about that space," said Thomas, "you're fired."

Years later, Thomas explained his reaction to Zambo's bulldogging: "A lot of people don't understand that higher up in the corporate ladder, a CEO is looking at a broad spectrum of issues. Yours is just one of 40 that will get his attention that day. The CEO picks the solution he wants, and you say, 'Fine.' Unless circumstances change, you don't bring it up again. And you never bring it up a third time unless you want your ass handed to you in a basket." (Especially, according to reputation, if the top dog getting that third request was Al Neuharth.)

Zambo wasn't about to self-destruct with a fourth call but neither was she giving up. It was time to bench determination and bring on imagination. On a clear day, Zambo took a professional photographer to the tower site. The topmost floors were already leased, so the pair ascended in the construction elevator to the 32nd floor, the highest still available. Zambo directed the photographer to make a visual record of the panoramic views from that commanding elevation, including the Lincoln and Jefferson Memorials, the Kennedy Center, even the Capitol. That evening, Zambo returned with the photographer to get on film views of the city aglow. "I wanted to show what Mr. Neuharth would see from his desk," says Zambo. The photographer was afraid of heights, especially in the dark, but with Zambo's firm encouragement, he completed his assignment.

A portfolio of the photos was sent to Thomas with a note from Zambo. It said,"If I can't bring you to the building, I'm bringing the building to you."

A few days later, Thomas phoned Zambo to say that Neuharth was coming to town and that he wanted him to see the Rosslyn tower. But not with a broker or the developer. Zambo was instructed to arrange for a construction elevator operator to be on call for three days and nights, ready to take Neuharth up to the tower's highest available floors.

Neuharth visited the building and promptly claimed it for *USA Today.* And he wanted the newspaper's name to be on the building. "The owner was unwilling to do that," says Zambo, "unless Gannett leased at least half the building." Gannett obliged, taking 258,000 square feet. "Their intention was to sublet much of that space," says Zambo, "but by the time they had moved in their people, they had very little left to sublet." Despite *USA Today*'s earlier rejection of a Virginia address, it now had one, so Zambo leased space on Capitol Hill, providing an appropriate mailing address for the nation's newspaper, much as the *Reader's Digest* uses Pleasantville, New York, even though its headquarters are in adjacent, less resonantly named Chappaqua.

In the mid-1980s, a second tower rose from the same base as the *USA Today* building. Zambo negotiated a lease in the new space for the Gannett Foundation, founded in 1930 in Rochester, New York. Its mission was then to fund hospitals and other public service institutions in places where Gannett published newspapers. In 1992, the foundation changed its name to Freedom Forum, in preparation for its new thrust into the media world.

The Newseum opened in 1997 as the only interactive museum dedicated to the First Amendment, to news gatherers, and to newsroom diversity. Despite its location in Rosslyn, well off the spine of intense tourist traffic along the Mall in Washington, the Newseum proved to be an increasingly popular attraction. By the end of 2000, it had hosted more than 1.5 million visitors. The Freedom Forum decided that it wanted to find a more central location for the Newseum and to double its size. "In my parlance, you fish where the fish are," explains Charles Overby, chairman of the Freedom Forum and once the editor of a Pulitzer-prize-winning newspaper in his native Mississippi.

"They had their 'starter' museum," says Zambo. "Now they were ready for a permanent site." With the Newseum's lease expiring in three years, time was of the essence.

Zambo was as well known to Freedom Forum as to *USA Today*. In the early 1990s, she'd been given the task of finding a midtown Manhattan site for the New York branch, then inconveniently located uptown at Columbia University. The Forum wanted multiuse space for exhibitions, conferences, and executive offices. Zambo partnered with Daniel Horowitz, a broker in Studley's midtown office, who prepared space reports on possible locations. Zambo, however, did the client contact.

"Lois showed us a map with landmarks enlarged and with 40 stickers representing potential sites," says Overby. "We narrowed it down to 12 and she said, 'Let's go look at them.'"

Zambo took the group to what Overby calls a "great" Rockefeller Center site, lacking only the column-free, unobstructed, open space necessary for filming Freedom Forum events. They ascended to the 42nd floor of an East Side office tower under construction. "Lois led the way out onto open gangplanks," says Overby. "Not everyone had the courage to follow." They did the same at a West Side tower so that Neuharth could see the view from what would be a high terrace, although at the time there was only a ledge-like place "for window washers."

Then Zambo showed her client a space newly vacated by IBM high up in Big Blue's 43-floor tower on Madison Avenue at 57th Street. "I didn't want to have my head turned by some great view," Overby admits, "but the former executive offices on the top floor blew us away." The difficulty was that the entire elevator bank from top down was being offered for rent. Overby only wanted the top floor and space below the lobby for Freedom Forum exhibitions. "We did the impossible by getting [owner] Ed Minskoff to rent us only what we wanted," says Zambo. But the negotiation was tough. "Ed called up Julien at one point," she says "and asked him to get me to go easier on him. Julien told Ed that he couldn't ask me *not* to fully represent my client."

"After that deal," says Overby, "Lois became Wonder Woman."

As Overby geared up late in 1999 to relocate the Newseum, he read a newspaper story about the renovation of an office building at 101 Constitution Avenue being leased by Studley. That address had both the right sound for a museum dedicated to the First Amendment and the perfect location: "catty-corner to the Capitol." Overby called Zambo, perhaps expecting that she would jump at this opportunity to make a major deal without having to do any legwork.

"No, Charles," said Zambo, "you don't want to be at 101 Constitution Avenue, even though our firm is the leasing agent. You'd be doing exactly what you're escaping from, which is shoe-horning yourself into an existing building."

Zambo now prepared an inventory of 30 potential downtown sites for the Newseum. "We looked at buildings near the Holocaust Museum and the Lincoln Memorial," says Overby. "The biggest problem was that they were on the registry of historic buildings. You couldn't alter the outside or even the inside. That ruled them out." The search focused on the former Woodward & Lothrup department store in downtown Washington, spacious and easily adaptable to a museum. It had the immense added advantage of being at a crossroads of the city's Metro lines. The drawback to the site, which took the sheen off its advantages, was the neighborhood's seediness. Even the arrival of the Newseum might not have changed that.

While the "Woodie's" site was for sale, another that was in a class of its own was not. "Charles, this is the one you're going to want," Zambo had said, as she pointed to it on the map. "But it's also the one that'll be hardest to get."

The site was a half block, covering 73,000 square feet, fronting on Pennsylvania avenue at Sixth Street, NW. For nearly 200 years, new presidents have paraded along the Avenue on their way to the White House after having been sworn in at the Capitol. The site runs the full depth of the block, backing onto "C" Street. Adjacent to it is the Canadian embassy. Across the avenue, the site faces the majestically proportioned National Gallery of Art. At the diagonal, one block away, is the National Archive, where the original First Amendment document is preserved.

This site would have leapt to first on Zambo's list if it could be bought. But that was far from the current reality. For one thing, the site was not even vacant. Since the 1960s, it had been the location of the Department of Employment Services (DES), a city agency doing job placement and training. In contrast to the architecturally ambitious, strikingly contemporary embassy next door, the DES building was a banality gone to seed. Here on the Mall, so highly public and ceremonial, it seemed misplaced in both design and function. As Zambo explained, it was the one location on the Mall between the Capitol and the White House that might be available for new development if DES could be moved elsewhere.

"We were told," says Overby, "that this was the most sought after property on the East Coast, then in the whole country. It was like the last oceanfront lot."

Transforming the DES site would also be the final act in an effort to upgrade Pennsylvania Avenue that went back to Inauguration Day, 1961. In the eighteenth century, Pierre l'Enfant had conceived of the avenue as a key axis of the city. But a goodly stretch of its north side never came close to grandeur. As Arthur Goldberg, JFK's new secretary of labor, rode in the 1960 inaugural parade, he observed "a bunch of decrepit pawn shops, taverns, horrible souvenir shops that took advantage of tourists, and second-hand clothing stores. In sum, it was a disgrace." (Quoted by Carol Highsmith and Ted Landphair in *Pennsylvania Avenue, America's Main Street,* and cited in "America's Main Street," by David Takesuye in *Urban Land,* October 2001.)

President Kennedy agreed with Goldberg that something should be done about Pennsylvania Avenue. He assigned the young, urban-savvy Daniel Patrick Moynihan, then an aide to Goldberg, to lead a task force to deal with the problem. Moynihan responded in June 1962, with a report finding that "increasingly, the Capitol itself is cut off from the most developed part of the city by a blighted area that is unsightly by day and empty by night." The report called for a "Pennsylvania Avenue that is lively, friendly, and inviting, as well as dignified and impressive."

Not until 1972 did Congress create, at the urging of Richard Nixon, the Pennsylvania Avenue Development Corporation (PADC). By 1996, the avenue had been upgraded to the point that the PADC could be disbanded. But there remained one blemish on the north side: the DES building. With Zambo's help, Overby was determined to replace it with a jewel.

The normal way for the city to dispose of a unique site, Zambo knew, would begin with a request for proposals (RFP) from any and all parties who had a plan and the means to develop it. Unknown to Zambo, in fact, the paperwork for an RFP for the site was actually being prepared by D.C. bureaucrats when she put it on her list for Overby. Going the RFP route was the way to get the most ideas into the design arena, and the best proposal might even be the one eventually selected. The drawback was the plodding time frame. First, the competing designs would be submitted and pondered. Once a winner was selected and financially qualified, years would pass, and the Newseum's lease in Rosslyn would have expired.

Other than that, the site was perfect. Overby estimated that it would draw 1 million visitors annually—triple the attendance in Rosslyn.

"We asked Lois if she could come up with a way to get the site by our deadline," says Overby. "She felt that if we did everything right we could get it—or at least be in the hunt. And she understood that the city wanted both the best use *and* the best price for the site. Usually, you can get only one or the other. So far, no developer had been able to get through that quagmire."

"We were prepared to go down either of two avenues," says Zambo. "One was to be ready and poised to jump in quickly when the RFP came out of the city. But so was everyone else in the world. I felt there had to be another way."

That other way was original and bold. Zambo proposed making Mayor Anthony Williams a preemptive offer for the DES site, one that he dare not refuse. The offer would be so rich that all other would-be bidders would back off. But it would be contingent on skipping an RFP competition and sealing the deal swiftly. Zambo also proposed to figure out which community activists might be against the Newseum coming to the Mall and proactively neutralizing any such opposition. If all went well, the Freedom Forum would own a key piece of the Mall a mere six months after the deal was broached.

"They asked if I'd ever done something like this before," says Zambo. "I told them no, but neither had anyone else. The city could say no, that's all."

Even if the mayor agreed to the deal without an RFP, approval also would have to come from the city council, the D.C. financial control board, and the federal Department of Labor, a co-owner of the DES building. Once the Freedom Forum's offer was put on the public table, others who coveted the site would also demand to be heard.

"Charles said to me," says Zambo, "'Lois, don't let me get outmaneuvered.'"

Without expert help on the political side, Zambo knew she might well get outmaneuvered. She turned first to Stephen Harlan, a former vice chairman of the all-important D.C. financial control board, which has oversight over the city budget. In that post, Harlan had hired Anthony Williams as the city's chief financial officer. Now that Williams was mayor, it was a good bet that he would be available when Harlan called. "I'd been introduced to Steve by a girlfriend at the Economic Club," says Zambo. "He told me that he'd never done anything like this, and he wasn't sure he could." Still, Harlan signed on. So did Edward M. Rogers of Nixon Peabody, who became lead lawyer in the effort, and Chris Brady, a veteran lobbyist. As a trio, the three men had deep contacts on Capitol Hill and in all levels of government. Zambo calls them her "dream team."

Zambo focused personally on the task of cultivating grassroots support for the Newseum relocation. "I'd been involved in a couple of deals that required zoning variances," she says. "I sat back and watched how the developers went about it. Mostly, they'd just try to jam it down on the community. These local people would get so disgusted that they would just downzone the project rather than upzone it. That could so easily have been prevented if the developer had just gone out and listened to the locals." Zambo sought out two community leaders: Charles Docter, chairman of Downtown Housing Now, and Terry Lynch, head of the Downtown Cluster of Congregations. "Terry had single-handedly held up the development of the old Garfinkel's department store site for three years," says Zambo.

Docter and Lynch were initially cold to the Newseum relocation. "Terry had made a negative comment to the *Washington Post,*" says Zambo, and Docter though the Freedom Forum was "some right-wing group." After the two activists toured the Newseum and met the staff, they warmed to the "mission," as Zambo puts it. Docter's suggestion that minority internships be created at the Newseum was accepted. As Zambo built a network of local support for the project, she "constantly called Terry and Charlie for advice."

And she promised them that their housing priorities would be part of the deal.

On May 10, 2000, Overby quietly opened the campaign for the Newseum relocation with an exploratory visit to the office of Jack Evans, chairman of the D.C. city council's finance and revenue committee. In an account of the meeting in the *Washington Times,* Evans said he was unfamiliar with the Newseum, other than knowing that it had been used for the filming of the season's final episode of his favorite TV show, "The West Wing."

"Another museum is not something I'm interested in," Evans told Overby. "I want something that will bring life to the site 24 hours a day." His suggestion: Add housing to the Newseum site, so that it would no longer be deserted at night. If that were done, Evans agreed to support the Newseum's move.

Pocketing Evan's promise, Overby returned to his office and called for an appointment with Mayor Williams. But the mayor insisted that Overby first meet with Eric Price, the city's economic development deputy. "I was a little put off by that," Overby told the *Times.*

On May 17, 2000, Overby hosted a dinner for Price and Andrew Altman, the city's planning director, at Arlington's Ritz-Carlton Hotel. Peter Pritchard, president of the Freedom Forum, also attended. Overby proposed a 531,000-square-foot building designed by James Polsheck, including a six-level Newseum and conference facilities with displays created by Ralph Applebaum, noted for his visuals at the Holocaust Museum. Also on site would be shops, a restaurant and about 100 condominium apartments. Despite the plan's ambition and the eminence of the architect, the city representatives were not wowed. Price pointed out that that nonprofit groups like the Freedom Forum paid no taxes.

"I don't think Eric was suggesting we should pay taxes. He was just stating a fact for our benefit," said Overby, according to the *Times.*

Point taken.

Clearly, city officials were underwhelmed by the prospect of the Newseum. But Overby and Zambo were planning an offer that would be hard to refuse.

The appraised value of the half-block site was $49 million. "I did a matrix of low and high sales prices based on every possible development scenario including offices, apartments, and a hotel," says Zambo. "If somebody—say, an investor from Japan or the Netherlands—wanted this site for a crown jewel, they might go to $60 million. Maybe, at the very outside limit, up to $70 million if they had money to burn."

Overby decided to blow away all competition with an offer of $75 million, more than a 50 percent premium over the appraised value. But he wasn't nearly done. Responding to Eric Price's concerns about yet another non-tax-paying foundation coming to town, Overby promised that the Newseum would pay full taxes. So would the condominium owners in perpetuity—even if ownership of the land changed.

Overby's package included one more potent incentive: If the city acted swiftly and sealed the deal by the end of 2000, Freedom Forum would throw in a $25 million bonus to be used for affordable housing at the mayor's discretion. On top of $75 million for the site, the offer came to a staggering $100 million.

"To me," says Overby, "that sounded like a magic number."

Flush times in the stock market allowed Overby to think extravagantly. By mid-2000, foundation assets, created in 1935 with a donation of $100,000 in Gannett stock from Frank Gannett, exceeded $1 billion. In short, the Freedom Forum could well afford to overpay for a Newseum site that was as rare, in its own way, as if an Old Master painting of quality was suddenly to appear on the market.

Zambo, always perfectly dressed and groomed, presented the Newseum plan at a Freedom Forum board meeting held in London in March 2000. "Normally, when I fly," she insists, "my make-up kit is the most important thing, so I carry it aboard. But I was so afraid that I'd lose my box of papers for the presentation that I carried it aboard. For the first time ever, I checked my make-up kit."

The flight arrived in London six hours late after being diverted to Wales. Overby had a taxi waiting for Zambo. That evening, she attended a dinner for Freedom Forum board members at the residence of the American ambassador. "Al Neuharth wanted to know how much the Canadian Embassy had paid for their site next to ours," says Zambo. That figure normally could be accessed from city records by her home office. But when she asked for it, word came back that, as a diplomatic transaction the information had not been recorded.

"Maybe Brian Mulroney can help us," suggested Overby. Canadian prime minister from 1984 to 1993, Mulroney was a trustee of the Freedom Forum, and he was on hand. "I'm presenting tomorrow," Zambo told Mulroney. "Could you can help me find out how much your embassy paid for its site on Pennsylvania Avenue?"

Mulroney promised to help, but when Zambo queried him in the hotel elevator the next morning, she remembers him saying, "Gee, it takes time to get that kind of information."

"I really don't have time," said Zambo. Before the end of the morning, Mulroney had provided her with the number that Neuharth wanted. "Later, I realized that, as former prime minister, Mulroney was like our former president. And here I was, saying, 'Hurry up and get me this number. . . . "

Zambo was given the signal to go after the DES site, although the details of the Freedom Forum's intention would not be made public for several months. Along with multiple hurdles that blocked the path to the Newseum's relocation, Zambo knew she would have to win over major developers who also might covet the site. Without an RFP process, they would never get the chance to go after it. One by one, Zambo convinced 15 developers to openly support the Newseum as the best use of the site and the best deal for the city—one that no commercial developer could come close to matching. Still, why would competitors come over to the Newseum's side? Perhaps in the hope of becoming a future development partner in the project. And that would happen.

While the Freedom Forum was in a hurry to strike a deal, Mayor Williams was not. Not yet, anyway. In early July 2000, Zambo told Overby, "I think we ought to push the mayor's back against the wall. Make him respond."

Overby agreed. He informed the mayor's office that the Freedom Forum would announce the Newseum plan at a press conference on July 11, 2000. "They asked us please not to do it," says Zambo. "But Charles said the news would get out anyway." The mayor rejected a request to appear at the press conference because he was planning to attend the All-Star baseball game in Atlanta that day. Zambo says that "when the mayor's office heard that both Lynch and Docter would be on hand at the press conference, he changed his travel schedule so that he could also be there."

By the time the press conference was held, on a rainy Tuesday in front of the DES building, the mayor seemed to have become a convert. "We are taking this offer very, very seriously," he said in a brief appearance before hurrying off to the airport. "We are going to move heaven and earth to get this done as quickly as possible." Within 45 days, the mayor promised, the city would review the Freedom Forum's $100 million offer and make a decision.

"When I heard the mayor talk about moving heaven and earth," said Overby later, "I felt we were on the way."

Zambo's bold effort to enlist key community leaders and developers had paid off. The *Washington Post*'s story on the event the next day quoted Terry Lynch as saying, of the Freedom Forum's offer, "it's like the District is winning the lottery." Charles Docter said the city "should waste no time in snapping up this bargain." And Mitchell Schear, president of Kaempfer Company, a major downtown developer who was also on hand, opined that the Freedom Forum's offer blew away the competition. "Not only are they paying big numbers," said Schear, "but they want to do it quickly. Nobody else could muster the money."

Zambo did not take Schear's opinion as gospel truth. What if some jealous developer decided to be a spoiler? Over the ensuing weeks, she continued to persuade additional major developers to write letters to the city council expressing their support for the Newseum. One of the most prominent, Oliver Carr, president of CarrAmerica, which had done major local development and coveted the site, wrote a letter to the editor of the *Post,* dated August 1, 2000, praising the Newseum plan. In time, Carr would get his payback.

"As a developer, I had intended to compete for the site," wrote Carr, "but the Freedom Forum plan addresses every goal set forth in the mayor's downtown action plan as well as those in the long-standing Pennsylvania Avenue Development Corporation's plan for the avenue." Besides paying "a price above market" and offering to pay commercial tax rates, Carr affirmed that "the Forum is ready to move quickly and has the resources and skills to deliver on its commitments."

Zambo hardly expected support from developers to be unanimous. "I made a list of developers likely to be the most unhappy," says Zambo, "but the one who protested the most was one we'd never thought of." A lawyer for that out-of-town developer, whom Zambo won't name, called her. "He asked me what the hell I was trying to do and insisted that the city couldn't possibly sell the site without an RFP."

"All you're asking for is a lawsuit," the lawyer told Zambo. "You tell your client to let the public process go forward." Zambo asked if his client planned a suit to stop the Newseum deal.

"Maybe."

"Why? Just to be a spoiler?"

Zambo called the developer directly and expressed her opinion that a suit would make him look "really, really bad."

"A few weeks later," she says, "the lawyer called to say that his client was going on to bigger and better things."

In an editorial supporting the Newseum offer in July, the *Post* asked, "Can the District conduct its due diligence and make a sound and timely decision within the next 45 days, as Mayor Williams has promised? We would hope so."

That hope was not in vain. The mayor moved "heaven and earth" even faster than promised. Just 30 days after the July press conference, he announced his endorsement of the deal. More than that, he had already struck an agreement with the federal Department of Labor, which had paid for the construction of the DES building, and still owned 67.3 percent of it. Without Labor's nod, no sale could occur. Alexis Herman, then secretary of labor, agreed to transfer the agency's ownership stake in the building to a new DES facility, to be built east of the Anacostia River in a neighborhood much in need of economic stimulus.

The next hurdle was the city council. "After the mayor announced his support," says Zambo, "a council member stood up in the chamber and said that she was personally opposed to any kind of procurement done on a noncompetitive basis." But the "dream team" worked the council well. All went swimmingly on October 16, 2000, when the council's committee on economic development held a public hearing on the proposed sale. Eric Price, who had been cool to Overby's offer in May, now testified that "it is difficult to conceive of a more generous offer that also satisfies the District's social, cultural, and planning objectives."

"I don't remember any other nonprofit that has agreed to pay taxes," added the chairperson, Charlene Drew Jarvis.

The hearing was going smoothly for Zambo. Too smoothly. Near its end, she was caught off guard when a distinguished-looking man rose and, identifying himself as an architect, offered a surprise proposal for the site: Since the Canadian embassy already occupied half the block, why not install the Mexican embassy on the other half? Then our "neighbors to the north and to the south" would share an equally prominent site. Currently, the architect pointed out, the Mexican Embassy was located at a less than prestigious site across from a dry cleaner.

"Was the Mexican government the gentleman's client?" asked chairperson Jarvis. The architect insisted that it was not. His purpose was only to send "a message about the greatness of Mexico."

Zambo, wearing a trim blazer in an oversized hound's tooth pattern and a dark skirt, was sitting in the front row with a Freedom Forum contingent led by Overby. She visibly tensed up at this "Mexican" initiative out of the blue. Although it came to nothing, it showed that even a highly alert broker could not foresee every twist.

In November, the council approved the deal, officially called the "Negotiated Sale of District-Owned Property at 500 C Street, N.W. to the Freedom Forum, Inc. Approval Resolution of 2000." Now the deal had to be okayed by the financial control board. "They weren't against it," says Overby, "just not enthusiastic. Least enthusiastic was the entrenched bureaucracy." But it had an incentive not to dither: If the deal wasn't approved by the end of the year, the city would have lost $25 million.

The city did not lose out. On December 21, 2000, in the mayor's ceremonial office, the deed to the Newseum's new site was signed over to the Freedom Forum. Fifty million dollars immediately was wired from Chicago Trust Company to the city's account. Twenty-five million dollars more would be transferred when DOS vacated the building in July 2001. The last $25 million would be released when building permits were issued to the Freedom Forum. Interest on all escrowed money would be shared equally between seller and buyer.

Demolition of the DOS building was completed on December 20, 2001. One year later, ground was broken to start construction of the Newseum and Freedom Forum headquarters. Its development partner is none other than Oliver Carr of CarrAmerica, who had earlier written to the *Washington Post* claiming he had not intended to compete for the site. The upshot is that instead of becoming a competitor, Carr became a partner. The Newseum's grand opening is planned for 2006.

Early in the spring of 2001, several months after Freedom Forum took title to the site, the Canadian embassy invited over its future neighbors. Overby brought Zambo. "We stood on a balcony on the top floor of the embassy," says Overby. "The Capitol was right on top of us and I looked at all the national monuments stretching right and left."

"Then I said, 'Lois, we didn't pay enough for what we got.' She just threw her head back and laughed."

9 Teaming

One broker's achievement is seen by outsiders as the entire company's achievement.

—Julien Studley

In 1980, Kurt Handschumacher, then a lanky and long haired 24-year-old in his second year at Studley, began using a tool that American astronauts also were using. It was the HP-41C, a state-of-the art, handheld calculator that was programmable and incorporated a thermal strip printer. It was priced at $325. A photo on the National Air and Space Museum web site of a smiling Sally Ride, astronaut on a Columbia voyage in 1983, shows an HP-41C at her side. It could calculate when a ground station was available to send or receive data. It could even do reentry calculations if main computers failed. Only 10 years earlier, the Apollo moonwalkers had to make do with slide rules. The HP-41C's main adaptation to space was a Velcro strap to keep it from floating away. Unlike the astronauts, Handschumacher was earthbound. But he did use the HP-41C to explore a new realm of brokerage service at Studley.

In traditional brokerage, the highest priority had always been to close the deal. The next priority was to avoid sharing the commission check. But Handschumacher's priority was analytical rather than transactional. He was then on a team of four brokers, formed by Don Schnabel, which voluntarily shared commissions on the deals they worked on together. The team's first client was U.S. Trust Company. The evolution of teams would profoundly alter the way Studley brokers reached out to clients. It also would cause the brokers to reach within the firm for the support of their colleagues. Teaming would change the culture of the firm.

"Way back in time, 99 percent of brokers were Lone Rangers," says Jacque Ducharme. Before he oversaw the building of seven teams in the Chicago office, including one of his own, Ducharme had done many deals as a Lone Ranger. "If two guys called themselves partners, the benefit was that one of them could be in the office to answer the phone if the other was canvassing," says Ducharme, who started at Studley in 1972. "But there was no particular division of skills. They were probably partners because they'd been high school buddies."

The need for diverse skills to be put at the service of a single client came about "when the language changed," says Nick Borg, who was Studley's chief operating officer until 2003. "Once the FASB [Financial Standards Accounting Board] came in back in the 1970s, brokers had to learn to speak "CFO-ese." Banks, law firms, corporations all had different needs, like whether to lease or own. Brokers needed to weigh tax issues, sale leasebacks, and changes in GAAP (generally accepted accounting principles). No longer were they doing real estate deals; they were doing financial deals."

Accounting firms and business consultants were equipped to handle the new financial issues posed by real estate. But if Studley brokers could provide comparable services, they also could go a step further. By gauging the psyches of landlords and tenants in real time, they could pick up early warnings of shifts in the market.

The chasm between a broker's savvy and an accountant's standardized tables yawned wide as Schnabel's team worked on behalf of U.S. Trust Company. The bank's accounting firm, for example, insisted that 770 Broadway, a full-block office tower built in 1906, in which the bank leased space, was nearing the end of its economic life. "According to their accounting tables, this building had a maximum life of 100 years," says Schnabel. "But 770 Broadway is still chugging along." It chugs along, in fact, with such up-to-date tenants as J. Crew and MTV.

The team examined various lease structures for U.S. Trust. "There are a couple of ways of classifying leases as operating or capital," says Handschumacher. "The bank had just finished doing a capital lease at 130 John Street. Ira Schuman [the only team member with an MBA] and I went through the flowcharts, looking at a whole lot of accounting issues. We took all the financial components of different leases, such as CPI [Consumer Price Index] and porters' wage escalation, and compared them using net present value of funds. And it turned out that the bank was better off doing an operating lease instead of a capital lease at 770 Broadway. It made a big difference on their books."

Schnabel had started out doing the computational work for U.S. Trust by laboriously pecking on a basic calculator. "I got to the point where the number crunching was taking me well beyond my comfort level and minutiae level with math," he says. That was when he turned to Handschumacher.

As a geology major who had worked in uranium mining, Handschumacher was not an obvious choice to carry out Schnabel's effort to the next level—except to Schnabel. "I did have a reasonable expectation that a man who had worked as a geologist must be familiar with how to measure the area of a parallelogram or trapezoid," he explains. "Those skills were transferable to calculations based on office floor plates."

Like his mentor, Handschumacher found himself "doing endless key strokes on a basic calculator." Then he switched to the newer HP-38E, which "eliminated all those key strokes, though it had to be constantly reprogrammed." A later HP model came along that could remember the program. Then came the "latest and greatest," HP 41-C, allowing Handschumacher to write 1000-line programs. The narrow tapes printed out from the back of the calculator were pasted down on pages that were photocopied for delivery to the client. Schnabel inspected each page to be sure it was perfect.

Closing the transaction is normally uppermost in the mind of any broker, because there is no payday without it. But the Schnabel team was paid an hourly rate rather than a commission by the client. At year's end, the team shared the proceeds according to a formula worked out by Schnabel.

Although the team mode is now mainstream at Studley, it is hard to overestimate how startling the concept was in the beginning. "We all knew that deals could be done on the back of an envelope," says Mike Solomon. "It wasn't rocket science. But once we needed to prove what was written there, we had to bring in an analyst. Now you have this guy who isn't in production, who doesn't even lift up the phone. There had to be a mental shift in brokers' thinking to: I am not only sharing my commission with people who can bring me into deals, but I am sharing with someone who can't bring me into a deal.

"The value was obviously there when the broker could show this snazzy work product to the client. But if the guy producing it could also speak in a salesman-like manner like Matt Barlow or Peter Capuciati [top number crunchers and earners on their respective midtown-based teams] . . . Wow! That made a difference. That put you ahead of the guy with an envelope and pencil. At first, there were only two or three people feeding this analyst. And so the idea of making teams bigger came into being."

Teaming as a Studley concept got a push in the mid-1980s as a byproduct of a spirited internal argument over whether to pursue national accounts. That was a new idea at the firm, which had made its reputation by honing the art of the one-off deal. The firm's expertise in law firm brokerage, for example, did not normally require a great deal of crisscrossing the country. This would be a requirement for representing a national chain of stock brokers or accounting firm branches.

The drive for national accounts was spearheaded from the Washington office by the veteran Peter Speier and Scott Pannick, then a new and ambitious broker. In a culture where offbeat talent had been valued more than conventional credentials, Pannick represented, as he puts it, "Studley's first foray into Harvard MBAs." Also pushing for a national front was Julie Schuelke, a newcomer to brokerage who came from a corporate background. "We said we wanted to do important things," says Schuelke. "We need the credibility to get hired by a CIGNA or an AT&T and to do all their business. We didn't want to be limited by happening to live in Washington, D.C. Teams were the nomenclature for doing all that."

Julien admits that he did not welcome the national accounts initiative. It required hiring midlevel people to service the new clients, as well as a steep increase in travel expenses. As it stood, branch offices paid for their own travel to get business. "The philosophy had always been, if you're a broker who thinks it's worth traveling to New Orleans in search of a deal, then you pay for it personally," says Nick Borg, "because we don't want to second-guess your entrepreneurship. If you make the deal, then we will reimburse a share of your expenses at the same rate as your commission share."

As national accounts started up, the travel bill had to be footed by headquarters rather than the broker. Higher overhead was anathema to Julien. He questioned the value of national work itself. Although some of it could be lucrative, other parts might not be worth the effort. "This kind of business is profitable for spurts of time," he says, "but you can get mired in small transactions and ultimately lose the account." Nick Borg says, "You'd be handling two dozen little deals in some backwater in order to get one big deal."

But the push for national accounts was not to be denied. It meant new, large-scale business, and Studley's client list grew to include Microsoft, Gateway, and an as-yet-untarnished Arthur Andersen. Such clients needed a spectrum of information that went beyond the norms of one-off deals, ranging from labor pool analysis to the long- term impact of road and airport construction at multiple sites. Even a "renaissance broker," accustomed to handling all aspects of big transactions, could not hope to cover all the bases for a national client. That required a team effort.

Studley did not need to get fatter in order to be successful at servicing national accounts, as Mark Jaccom's "lean and mean" team forcefully demonstrated. Jaccom, an aggressive business getter and now also vice chairman in charge of national accounts, arrived at Studley in 1990. He quickly hired Peter Capuciati, a math whiz who says he had planned to be a graduate student in plasma physics at Columbia University until his research grant was canceled. Capuciati, looking for a job, answered Studley's listing for an analyst posted at the university employment office.

Jaccom's team, consisting of himself and Capuciati as his "chief brainiac" (as Borg calls him), prides itself in delivering sophisticated data to national clients who must relocate to existing or build-to-suit offices. Since the team competes directly with MBA-heavy consulting firms, it must get the job done faster and cheaper, adding the firm's trademark bonus of ear-to-the-ground market smarts.

Unlike other teams, which develop in-house analytic talent, the Jaccom team outsources technical work and tries to pinpoint issues that go well beyond the real estate. It steered a California client away from a potential expansion site, for example, after learning of future freeway interchange construction sure to cause years of traffic delay. For another client seeking to locate amid a high concentration of registered nurses, the Jaccom team arranged with the state nursing association to purchase the residential zip codes (but not the names) of its members. That list guided the client's location decision.

It might seem that the best solo brokers would shy away from the team concept. Why share earnings if they already can "do it all?" When Jacque Ducharme headed the Chicago office, he didn't feel that way, even though he'd single-handedly done deals as complex as the siting and construction oversight of the University of Chicago's downtown business school as part of a PUD (planned unit development) along the Chicago River. Ducharme formed his office's first team 17 years ago. "You don't see very many one-man football teams," Ducharme explains. Commission sharing works out because "Lone Rangers might keep $100,000 on a deal, but we on the team are keeping $1 million."

As on the court, it sometimes makes sense to double- or even triple-team to win the deal. In a transaction completed in 2001, a trio of Chicago teams combined to find a solution to the space needs of the American Bar Association. Largest of all national voluntary professional organizations, the ABA for years had long divided its national headquarters between a pair of buildings on the fringe of the central city. Four blocks apart, they had ample parking and hotel choices but lacked convenient public transportation. Administration was centered in one location, back office in the other. Although management assumed that the bifurcation was efficient, an intensive, three-month-long Studley "city planning" study showed that the benefits were illusory.

"We found that they were running T-1 lines between the buildings and up their spines, which is an expensive proposition," says John Goodman, captain of one of the teams and a Chicago branch manager. "They also had messengers running back and forth. And getting people together from the two locations for meetings was no easy task."

With its lease not expiring until 2004, the ABA had commissioned Studley to study its situation in the spring of 1999. But it was not ready yet to send a broker out looking for new space. That was fine with Studley. "We always try to figure out how to develop relationships with the client before it becomes a beauty contest," says Goodman. "Our inclination is to start talking to them well before their lease is up."

Augmenting Goodman's team on the assignment was a team co-captained by Jacque Ducharme and Joe Learner. A third team, specializing in construction and technology, was led by architect Richard Dale. For three months, team members interviewed their ABA counterparts on a range of issues including finance, technology, marketing, demographics, law, and accounting. Goodman says, "We'd put the results up on boards and ask, 'Are we properly capturing your business objectives?' We did that until our team of consultants mirrored their team of internal experts."

The next phase was guided by what Laurie Condon, coordinator of the three teams, describes as a "seven-point standard deviation model that objectified client goals, including long-term financial impact, accessibility to labor, property management, and image. We weighted them and scored them and said, 'These are your decision drivers.'"

A complicating factor, according to Goodman, was that the ABA's top management was not autonomous. "They were constrained by what they might have chosen and what they thought their membership demanded, as represented by the ABA's real estate committee and the board of governors. They were faithful stewards who did not want a new home that would be perceived as too flashy."

The ABA leaned toward constructing its own headquarters building. Studley identified a promising, mixed-used site to be developed over the Illinois Central railroad tracks between Lake Michigan and Michigan Avenue. "We deeply developed a proposal for a building which would be 70 percent owner-occupied by the ABA," says Goodman. "We knew it could be financed, and it was a great location next to a train station."

Four hundred thousand members strong, the ABA certainly rated its own office tower. But Joe Learner's analysis showed that the building would have to be taller than the ABA wanted in order to achieve financial efficiency. "The land costs a certain amount, and construction costs a certain amount, and you don't have that much leeway," says Learner. "And once you build your premises, you cannot grow or shrink it as you need." Also on the downside was the ABA's for-profit status. Any building it owned would be taxed.

Trying hard to keep its prime tenant, the owner of the larger of the ABA's two current buildings offered to expand and restack the premises. Ninety percent of the ABA's staff could then be in under one roof. But consolidation would not bring easy access to mass transportation, an issue hindering the organization's ability to recruit and keep its labor force. "Labor costs," says Goodman, "can be five to ten times the cost of your real estate."

The teams had scouted existing space in downtown Chicago, but the ABA needed a minimum of 200,000 square feet, and that was hard to find. The Quaker Tower at 321

North Clark Street, on the Chicago riverwalk, did beckon. With a major law firm and Quaker Oats itself moving out, suitable space would be available. But the tower's Japanese owner had been uncooperative. Studley tried but failed to strike a deal to put the ABA there.

But then, in April 2000, Quaker Tower was purchased jointly by Houston-based Hines and a New York–based pension fund. The new owners were eager to snare the ABA as their first major new tenant. On the eve of a meeting of the ABA's real estate committee to consider a different deal, Hines made an eleventh hour offer at below-market rent. Six months later, the lease was signed. The ABA took 225,000 square feet in the tower, 185,000 on upper floors and 40,000 at or below ground level dedicated to data, printing and mailing operations. The staff will also have use of a private terrace over the Chicago riverwalk. ABA got other key benefits, including options to expand, contract, or sublease, and even the right to replace the management agent.

Just when it seems that a lone broker will get flattened by an aggressive, multiskilled team in the competition for a big deal, the unexpected happens. While the ABA was being triple-teamed in Chicago, a broker named Steve Grill was working quietly and alone with SFX Entertainment, which calls itself the nation's largest producer of live entertainment. Spun off in 1998 from SFX Broadcasting (SFX is radio shorthand for sound effects), the company sought its own quarters. Grill found the company an entire building clad in terra cotta at 220 West 42nd Street. Called the Candler Building, it was built by Coca-Cola kingpin Asa Griggs Candler in 1914. At the low ebb of the Times Square district, the building had been completely vacant. Renovated and restored, it is now on the National Register of Historic Places. Grill netted a commission of around $2 million on the deal. He had no team to share it with. During his first 10 years at Studley, the former tennis instructor had not distinguished himself as a big earner. Julien once told Grill that he would "eat my hat" if Grill ever had a million-dollar year. After the SFX Entertainment deal was done, a bowler hat on a plate was delivered to Julien's office—made of chocolate.

Grill's coup is the exception to the rule that even the most skilled lone broker cannot hope to match the response of a well-tuned team, especially when speed counts. In Washington, for example, a seven-person team headed by Tom Fulcher and Steve Goldstein got an urgent request from a large local law firm for "help in understanding our real estate situation." Exactly six days after delivery of the firm's existing lease to Studley, the team did a multimedia presentation to the lawyers' real estate committee. It included a 40-page analysis of that lease and a graphic display of the firm's large office building, showing each tenant's space layout and lease expiration. Another display mapped the locations of the city's 100 largest law firms. Various growth and attrition rates for the firm were presented.

The team even corrected management's assumption that it was allotting 600 square feet per lawyer. After discounting unusable space, it was more like 800 square feet—a one-third increase in per capita expense. The lawyers listened intently to that. Even small differences in per-person space allotments loom large at law firms because, after salaries, office space is typically the largest expense.

"Our presentation blew them away," says Fulcher. But it did not snag the client. Not then, anyhow. But if the partners were to decide to move to new space, they know whom to call.

Teams have aligned in unlikely ways, like Washington's odd-couple partnership of Julie Schuelke and Bill Quinby. Schuelke came to Studley with a management background and specializes in working with law firms. Quinby trained as an architect and is an expert in the slow moving world of university construction. Schuelke works mainly on the East Coast, while Quinby has focused on California colleges. Yet the pair has built a successful seven-person team: five partners and two salaried analysts. "The object of teaming with Bill was to smooth out the financial bumps," says Schuelke. "People who work individually may get a big payoff and keep it all. But it might be four or five years before it happens again. We're like a law firm in the sense that, regardless of what we are each doing, we all benefit from the same pot." In 2002, a difficult year for commercial real estate, Schulke and Quinby took home identical earnings and shared fifth place on the list of Studley's top earners.

The task of dividing earnings among team members is delicate. "That's where the rubber meets the road," says Mitch Steir, who built Studley's highest earning team on his way to succeeding Julien as chairman. "The street is littered with people who say, 'If it weren't for me, this or that deal would never have happened.' Other people will say that an analyst can only be worth X or a consultant can only be worth Y. When Mattie Barlow earned over $1.5 million in a year, there was a certain mindset within the company which asked: How can you pay an analyst that much money? But we are all delivering whatever we bring to the table. The idea is to keep every deal on track and to keep everyone motivated."

Steir arrived at Studley in 1988 after leaving Huberth & Peters, an old-line firm that, under inept new ownership, was foundering. Only after an agreement to join Cushman & Wakefield fell through did the 28-year-old Steir end up at Studley. "When I told people where I was going," he says, "it was a quasi-unpleasant experience for me. I kept being told that this was a sleepy shop." No great notice was taken at the arrival of the slender, boyish new broker from a Boston suburb, even though he'd won the real estate board's "Deal of the Year" award in his second year at his old firm. Probably the only person who sensed that Steir was marked for stardom as a broker was himself. And he did not intend to do it as a solo act.

Steir wasted no time in constructing his team. A key early hire was Matt Barlow, fresh out of college. David Goldstein, a musician as well as a broker, joined the team in 1991. A year later, Steir snared Michael Colacino, a Harvard graduate with wide cultural interests as well as advanced math skills. Before arriving at Studley in 1991, Colacino had been a principal in a small business consulting firm with some large clients, including Merrill Lynch and Metropolitan Life.

In 1988, Colacino analyzed a group of run-down office buildings in Manhattan newly purchased by Harry Macklowe, a developer who had started with Studley in the 1950's. "These buildings needed some love," says Colacino. Macklowe had paid $200 million for them. One year later, after minor upgrading, he sold them for $300 million. A profit of $100 million in a single year! Real estate brokerage, Colacino decided, was the place to be, even though "we all wanted to grow up to be writers and doctors." Hoping to be a science fiction writer, Colacino had read 2000 books as a boy. " I guess I was too scholarly." he says. " because I was best at analyzing all the plots." A client once jokingly said to Colacino that he wouldn't do business with anyone who could not quote Chaucer. Whereupon, Colacino began to recite "The Canterbury Tales."

Steir, an edgy gladiator in the deal-making arena, foresaw great synergy if the more contemplative, yet incisive Colacino could be lured to his team. In a bold gamble, he guaranteed Colacino that he would soon be making a seven- figure income if he joined up. It was a gamble that paid off. The trio of Steir, Barlow, and Colacino became the core of a team that, between 1995 and 2000, would grow to 14 members including junior "cold callers." It was the largest of any Studley team. It that period, it generated total commissions of more than $90 million.

Steir is known for his "lucky shoes," which he wears to crucial presentations. The story is told that, as Steir was walking on Fifth Avenue on the way to visit a key prospect, he suddenly realized that he'd forgotten his lucky shoes. A call was put in to his office to retrieve the shoes. They had not arrived by the time Steir reached the client's office. As he started his presentation, an assistant rushed in and said, "Here are your lucky shoes, Mr. Steir."

In 1996, Steir's team snagged a modest consulting assignment that evolved into a tenant representation deal that, even by Manhattan standards, would be titanic. It was also a standard-setting exercise in "repping the tenant." The client was Time Warner, whose divisions, ranging from small to enormous space users, were dispersed citywide. Among them were the magazine and book units of Time Inc., HBO, CNN, Turner Broadcasting, and the film and music units of Warner Brothers. The media giant's locally leased space totaled 3.5 million square feet. Yet management dealt piece-meal with its space needs. "You'd have one unit wanting 40,000 square feet and another unit looking to get rid of 40,000 square feet," says Steir, "and the twain would never meet." In all, Time Warner had 70 separate leases in the city.

"We were retained to organize all their lease data," says Barlow, "which was not only decentralized but not even automated. Our first task was to create a portfolio database with all key dates and to make strategic recommendations. And to get everyone to communicate with each other to establish best practices. We also wanted them to start acting like a major user of space. Here was this 3.5-million-square-foot whale that thought like a minnow with each deal rather than leveraging off of who they were."

The Steir team showed Time Warner how it could act like a whale in a deal it had completed for *Entertainment Weekly*. The magazine occupied two floors at 1675 Broadway, a tower owned by the Rudin family. *EW*'s lease was a few years from expiration in a tightening market for space-seekers. Despite "a window that was rapidly closing," the Steir team was able to negotiate new long-term leases for *EW* that actually cut its rent by $20 per square foot, a dramatic 40 percent reduction from its old rent.

How was that deal struck in a building that was already fully rented? "We emphasized to the Rudins that this tenant had the best credit in the building," explains Steir. "It was also the family's only link to this major corporation."

Those inducements alone were not enough to get the deal Steir wanted. "The Rudins told us our client could not move anywhere else in midtown for less rent, so why should they do it?" Steir countered with his "stalking-horse alternative." Rather than pay too high a rent, his client would opt to move into "backfill" space available elsewhere in the Time-Warner domain at below-market rents. "If that happened," says Steir, "in a few years, Rudin would lose its link to the city's largest publishing company."

Was that a creditable threat? "The landlord has the ability to see what your relocation possibilities are out there in the open market," says Steir. "But he can never see inside your backfill space portfolio. In a company as big as Time Warner, that could be wide and deep."

Entertainment Weekly's new 12-year lease for 50,000 square feet at 1675 Broadway was announced early in 1997. Over the lease term, *EW* will save millions of dollars. "This was the first time," says Barlow, "that we were able to show Time Warner how being a large corporation could benefit a small transaction."

About the time the *EW* lease was signed, its parent, Time Inc., a division of Time Warner and the country's premier magazine publisher, was wrestling with a severe office space crisis. Since 1959, the company had been headquartered in the Time & Life Building, a 48-floor tower at 1271 Avenue of the Americas in Rockefeller Center West. Although it was not generally known, Time Inc. was an original equity owner in the building, but sold its share in 1986 to the

Rockefeller Group. When the building was new, such flagship magazines as *People, Sports Illustrated, Entertainment Weekly,* and *InStyle* were yet to be born. The company's still growing stable of magazines had long since overflowed the 1.3 million square feet it occupied in the Time & Life Building. It was time to deal with the problem.

Time Inc.'s management invited an array of consulting and real estate firms to bid on a study of how to deal with its headquarters tower space crisis. Studley was not among them. The likely front runner was Cushman & Wakefield, which had long claimed Time Inc. as a client. The relationship between broker and client remained intact even after Cushman & Wakefield was bought by Rockefeller Group, Time Inc.'s landlord. As broker for both landlord and tenant, could Cushman & Wakefield represent Time Inc. without any conflict? Studley certainly could do that. Invited or not, Steir decided that his team had nothing to lose by "trying to get invited to the dance."

At 8 o'clock on the Friday evening marking the close of the competition, Mitch Steir called Joe Mayfield, a Time Inc. senior vice president who was working late. Steir reminded Mayfield of Studley's previous good work on behalf of *EW* and asked for the chance to bid on the new study. Mayfield relented. If Studley submitted a single-page proposal on Monday morning, it would be considered. Steir, Barlow, and Colacino worked over the weekend on the proposal. The team was then invited to make a formal presentation. Three weeks later, the assignment was Studley's.

"Time Inc. had the perception that they needed a lot more space—as much as 400,000 to 500,000 square feet," says Colacino. "Our competitors probably would have saluted and gone looking. But our response was, well, maybe you do need all that extra space. Maybe you don't. When we looked at their building, we realized that, while it gave the appearance of being jammed, in fact, the use of space was poorly planned. From a broker's viewpoint, our feeling was counterintuitive: Maybe they could stay put."

The team, working with space planning consultant Kelly, Legan & Gerard, looked hard at the 45-year-old Time & Life Building. "Each magazine had its own identity and felt it needed unique space to express that," says Colacino. "So the unit was the magazine and not the office. But the unit should be the office, because space is fungible, not identity. We told them that if you can just regularize systems throughout the entire building, you can grow within the building by 20 percent."

Then there was the "churn rate," or cost of redoing offices to reflect a magazine's identity. "They'd dream up a new magazine," says Barlow, "and they'd push somebody else out of the space they needed and then the editor would decide how to furnish it." Churn was costing Time Inc. an estimated $6 million annually. The team felt that cost could be reduced by 75 percent. The constant pressure on editors and writers to get magazines out, or what Colacino calls the "deadline cult," also contributed to the problem. "It's not the job of journalists to be introspective about real estate," he says.

At Time Inc.'s invitation, Studley now moved from the conceptual exercise in strategic planning to the art of negotiating for the tenant. The lease on the Time & Life Building was still almost a decade away from expiration. But, like a supertanker, a tenant in need of more than 1.5 million square feet of rental space needs to maneuver with ample lead time.

"We met with the landlord," says Barlow, "and told him that we were thinking about our options. The premises were old and tired. We guessed we could rebuild, but by the time that was done, the lease would be almost up, so we might as well look elsewhere to satisfy our client's need."

Rockefeller Group replied that it would be happy to extend the lease, but with the midtown office market definitely in the early phase of strengthening, it would never reduce the rent "by even one penny." The team did not take that assertion at face value. "We told them," says Colacino, "that we were starting a strategic activity that was commencing immediately and would end shortly. A decision would be made that could result in the owner having an empty building in nine years. That building would then be 45 years old and in need of an expensive retrofit to bring it up to standard. It could be empty for a very, very long time."

No owner could discount that threat. In the team's view, this owner was especially alert to risk. The majority stake in Rockefeller Group was held by Tokyo-based Mitsubishi Realty Trust. Japanese owners typically look to the long term and put a high premium on certainty. Colacino saw the situation in "deterministic" terms: "In nine years, what is inevitable can be discounted back to today, whereas uncertainty cannot be discounted."

Now that each side had made its opening thrusts, negotiations could begin in earnest.

"We started by doing our traditional stalking of the marketplace," says Colacino. The team eyed a 1.5 million-square-foot building at 1166 Avenue of the Americas, a few blocks from the Time & Life Building. It also considered a new tower being constructed by Morgan Stanley at 745 Seventh Avenue at 49th Street. After 9/11, the building was "flipped" to Lehman Brothers, which never moved into its damaged new headquarters at 1 World Financial Center. Steir's team then secured the top floors of that space for Cadwalader, Wickersham & Taft, the nation's oldest law firm—a key event in the revival of Lower Manhattan (see Epilogue).

The Steir team's hunt for a new home for Time Inc. was real, but it was also meant to persuade Mitsubishi that the magazine megalith was serious about the possibility of vacating its longtime home, even though its preference was to stay put. Still, even with a potential gain of 300,000 square feet from restacking, Time Inc. would still need more space. Steir's team did not have to look far to find it.

Next door to the home tower, at 135 West 50th Street, was a 700,000-square-foot tower named for its original anchor tenant, the American Management Association. The AMA was long gone, having moved further west to Broadway. The building it left behind, despite its key location, was debt-ridden and quite possibly headed for bankruptcy. Upkeep was minimal. "You heard it called the trailer park on West 50th Street," says Steir.

The attraction of the AMA building was its potential to help solve Time Inc.'s space problem. If a portion of this next-door neighbor could be leased while the team was renegotiating the "mother ship" lease, the two buildings might even be connected by an interior passageway. The team also saw the potential for what Colacino calls a "high floor, low floor arbitrage." Time Inc. could sublease the upper floors of the prestigious Time & Life Building for top dollar while taking advantage of cheaper space on the lower floors of the AMA building.

The tricky part of parallel negotiations would be to persuade Rockefeller Group that, even as Time Inc. took space in the AMA building, it might still move the bulk of its magazines from the Time & Life Building. Steir took the position that his client would only use the AMA building as "swing space" while the search for a new location went on. Various stratagems were used to make that search appear to be in earnest. "We had a sort of black box," says Steir. "I had to keep the spin nimble and vague enough so that I could redirect the black box from time to time. When Time Warner announced its Coliseum project, I said that now the strategy would be to move out all the magazines from Time & Life and brand them individually. They could be relocated anywhere. So instead of swing space, the AMA building would become home to one of the magazines. And we'd probably put *Time* magazine at the Coliseum site. Administrative people, we'd move down to CNN headquarters in Atlanta. All this was put on the table even though it was the client's desire to keep the magazines pretty much under one roof."

The team decided to try first to nail down about 200,000 square feet in the AMA building while working on the far bigger and more difficult Time & Life Building lease renewal. A complication was that the AMA building, owned by Dr. Lazlo Tauber, a Washington, D.C., physician and real estate magnate, was widely seen as being headed for foreclosure. "We knew that Tauber had to be financially viable in order for our tenant to be happy in his building," says Colacino. "So Matty [Barlow] did a financial analysis which caused us to be able to reverse engineer the building's mortgage and underlying ground lease so that we could set our lease payments to the exact point at which they would restore the AMA building's financial viability. We also had an engineering study of the premises done.

Julien Studley's direct dealings with Dr. Tauber over the AMA building went back to the 1960s. He had installed the AMA in the brand new building at 135 West 50th Street. Ten years later, Julien renegotiated a lease extension for the AMA, but a dispute over the commission on that deal soured Studley's relationship with Tauber. "What made our deal happen this time," says Colacino, "was that Tauber hired ESG [a Studley competitor] to market the building, and Mitch knew these people well and could work with them. He showed ESG our analysis of how, with Time Inc. as a major tenant, the building could be pulled out from under water."

The possibility of linking the AMA and Time & Life buildings via an internal passageway presented a ticklish problem. The team had told the Rockefeller Group that its client only planned to use the AMA building for swing space. Why then undertake to connect the buildings? "The decision was to leave that issue for last, and get all the critical path stuff done first," says Colacino. "At the very end of the negotiation, you kind of sweep in and say, 'Oh, by the way, we'd like to create this passageway.' By then, both sides are at the point of mutual exhaustion and you just want to get the deal done. It takes nerves of steel to go that route, but it worked."

Along with the new passageway connecting the buildings directly above their lobby levels, the team also wangled another last-minute benefit from Tauber: the right to rename 135 West 50th Street. "We didn't know which magazine wanted its name on the building," says Colacino. "So we just wrote the owner a letter saying we intended to name it. We didn't say what name it would be."

Time Inc. signed a 10 year lease for 220,000 square feet at 135 West 50th Street in October, 1998. Comparable midtown space was renting for $55 per square foot and rising, yet the deal was sealed on an "as is" basis for less than $35 per square foot.

"Michaelangelo said that the sculpture was inside the stone," says Colacino, "and that he was just removing pieces of it to let the sculpture out. Mitch works the deal that way. In a real estate deal, there are all these levels of posturing. Mitch strips away all the bullshit and uncovers the real transaction in all its clarity. That's his art."

With the AMA deal done, the team focused full attention on the Time & Life Building negotiation. "Things started quite unpropitiously," says Colacino. "The landlord thought there was going to be an upward reset of the rent midway in the client's current lease. With the escalation of operating expenses and taxes, the rent was anticipated to go from about $30 to $50 per square foot. But Matty Barlow had read all 70 lease documents linearly. Normally, nobody takes the time to do that. 150 pages apart, he found contradictory language that, closely read, gave us a creditable argument for a significantly less fruitful increase going to the landlord. That empowered our client to think aggressively. They needed to believe in their own case. Once the landlord senses that, you get accommodation.

Teamwork had brought the process well along. But it was Steir who finally faced the landlord alone in the role of deal closer. Even Joe Ripp, Time Warner's chief financial officer, who had worked closely with the Studley team, was not on hand. "For the tenant not to be in that room," says Colacino, "requires a leap of faith. By being in there alone, Mitch could do whatever was necessary to test the edges of what was a billion-dollar relationship. The result was extra savings for the client."

A 10-year lease restructuring for 1,538,000 square feet of space at the Time & Life Building, one of the largest ever on behalf of a single tenant, was signed in the spring of 1999. It included two five-year extension options which, if exercised, meant that Time Inc. had a home at least through 2027. Rockefeller Group agreed to carry out a multimillion dollar upgrade of the building's lobby and plaza. Steir estimates that the restructured lease, combined with municipal incentives negotiated by his team, "puts savings of at least $120 million in Time Inc.'s pocket" over the term of the lease. A pretty penny.

Further savings would have been realized if the proposed restacking of the Time & Life Building had been carried out. But that enterprise fell victim to the unrepentant (and often messy) individualism of magazine journalism. Next door, the planned branding did occur. The logo of *Sports Illustrated* is now on the former AMA building. A sleekly designed three-floor portal connects the two properties.

Few, if any of the team members involved with the deal knew that Julien's history with the AMA went back to the prehistory of the firm, when deal making was fashioned with the equivalent of Stone Age tools.

One of those tools was the penny postcard. Each evening after work at L.V. Hoffman & Co., the brokerage where he apprenticed, Julien returned to his bachelor apartment on East 53th Street and addressed those postcards to potential clients. Each one asked, "Can I help you find office space?" If the answer was yes, the respondent had only to tear off a prestamped return postcard addressed to Julien.

A penny postcard, in this age of clever mass mailings might seem like a quaint and unpromising way of getting business. But Julien did receive a response from the AMA, based in the green-clad McGraw-Hill tower on West 42nd Street. As Julien recalls, the AMA was in the market for 7,000 square feet of back office space. Actually, the client ended up taking 13,000 square feet in a building on West 44th Street.

The commission on that first AMA deal was measured in thousands of dollars, although to Julien it might as well have been millions. But that was not the only difference between then and now. Julien had done all the parts of that deal alone, from addressing the card to getting the client to drawing up the lease.

Nobody dreamed of teams back then. By 2003, as Julien was about to pass leadership of Studley to the next generation, the various offices of the firm could count upwards of 20 teams. But Julien remarked that he saw that number being reduced back to one. "Ultimately," he said, "I see the company becoming a single team."

10 Big to Small, Except for the Money

You're good enough to create opportunities if you don't get stuck with last year's problems.

—Julien Studley

"See those two apartment buildings up there?" asked Julien, one Tuesday morning, pointing from the rear seat of his blue Mercedes sedan. We were stuck in traffic on a highway cutting through the Bronx along the Harlem River. The pair of drab, eight-story buildings, high on an escarpment to our right, were in a neighborhood called Kingsbridge. It is the sort of blue-collar patch of the Bronx that Manhattanites who have trekked the Great Wall in China and glaciers in Patagonia don't know exists and probably never will.

"I own those two buildings," said Julien, "and all because of a $25,000 gamble I made 40 years ago. It was a really scary thing for me to put up that much money then. I'll tell you the story and you'll learn how money gets made in real estate."

There was time enough for what grew from story to mini-saga. Julien's regular chauffeur, Thach Chu, was taking him to New Paltz, New York, for an eleven o'clock meeting at the town hall. On the agenda was a discussion of how to create much-needed affordable housing in the town, two hours north of Manhattan. Julien's weekend house and the barn where he holds his annual apple festival are in New Paltz. Julien had been asked to attend the meeting by Jane Valez, director of Palladia, formerly known as Project Return, a private human services agency whose programs include housing. Julien is a board member of Palladia.

In Julien's telling, an odd thing happens: As the money gets bigger, the property generating it gets smaller. And although the action remains in New York, the location diverges from midtown Manhattan out to that remote corner of the Bronx. Still, the money keeps on growing. What drove the decisions at each juncture of deal making is the tax code. Understood by few, its arcane pages take an unusually forgiving attitude toward the appreciation of real estate value. The day of reckoning may eventually come, but it can be postponed for a lifetime. Annual earnings from that real estate, of course, are not immune to taxes. "I always pay the most taxes I can," Julien says. "If I overpay, I'll get a refund."

The core business at Studley has always been leasing office space rather than doing investment deals. Getting a lease signed may take months or years, but once it is done, the commission payoff is usually swift and may even be a lump sum. Investment deals move to a different rhythm. In the one Julien describes, profit accretes slowly. Money is taken out over decades, but these proceeds are classified as debt rather than profit, which is why the tax collector must cool his heels.

The action begins in 1963, when Julien took his gamble on the future direction of office tower development in midtown by purchasing a 90-day option on a pair of small buildings at the northwest corner of Third Avenue at 52nd Street. His hope was to find a developer who would buy up the entire blockfront up to 53rd Street for construction of a new office tower one block from the future site of the Citicorp assemblage (see Chapter 5). The seller of the option on the two properties, Fred H. Hill, then controlled all seven buildings on the blockfront. By optioning the corner to Julien, Hill was effectively becoming his partner. If Julien could find a buyer, they would both profit.

Julien's bet on Third Avenue came amid a spurt of office construction in Manhattan, driven partly by good times, but also by a change in 1961 in the city's zoning code. The old law, in force since 1916, had required tower facades to have setbacks as they rose, like multitiered wedding cakes. That law was a reaction to the advent of overbearing, sidewalk-darkening new office towers in Lower Manhattan, their verticality made possible by the advent of steel skeleton construction. The Equitable Building (completed 1915) at 120 Broadway, massing 1.2 million square feet on a site of less than an acre, was the prime culprit. Under the 1916 resolution, office towers could, and usually did, extend to the sidewalk line. But the wedding cake profile imposed on architects came to be resented by them. Le Corbusier's fresher vision (even if it had been around since the 1920s) of crisp modernist towers, hygienically isolated in open space, seemed like a better way to go. Mies van der Rohe's Seagram Building and its immaculate plaza, completed in 1958, was the movement's midtown beacon.

The stand-alone tower paradigm was reflected in the Zoning Resolution of 1961. It required developers to provide public plazas in exchange for floor height bonuses. But, so long as construction began within 12 months after passage of the new zoning resolution, building under the 1916 law was still permitted until 1962. The result was a rush of "old law" building starts that made 1961 the city's busiest year ever for office tower construction.

This being Manhattan, each new midtown tower had to be built on a plot where other buildings first had to be purchased and removed. It was difficult and expensive to assemble such sites. Park Avenue was considered the best address for office towers, with Fifth Avenue a close second. Then came Madison and Lexington Avenues. Third Avenue came on strong as tower territory after the removal of the last remains of the street-hogging and dirtying Third Avenue elevated subway line in 1956. The avenue's roadbed was then widened from 60 to 70 feet, 10 feet wider than either Madison or Lexington Avenues. What remained, at least temporarily, were the bars, delicatessens, and shops with walk-up apartments above. Third Avenue was especially famous for its antique and second handshops.

By the early 1960s, new office towers were already rising on Third Avenue in the East 40s. One of them, the 38-floor U.S. Plywood Building at No. 777, was completed in 1963, the year Julien bought his option on 52nd Street. That bulky tower had actually slipped into construction in 1961, under the old zoning rules. It rose above a distinctive early modernist townhouse, designed by the noted architect William Lescaze for his own home at 211 East 48th Street. Clearly high-rise development was headed up the avenue.

Fred Hill, with whom Julien placed his bet on the corner of 52nd Street, was known in real estate circles as an "operator," a type no longer active on the New York scene. Operators were quick-witted traders rather than developers or builders. "These guys might buy an option on a property on Monday and sell it by Friday," says Stan Kovak, a 40-year Studley veteran and advisor on property investments. "It wasn't in their plan to actually close on a property. Quite a few of them had offices at 565 Fifth Avenue, a building erected in 1921 and totally revamped in 1993. The main action was in the morning, and in the afternoon, they'd sit around playing cards."

Hill himself says, "I always liked the action. Once, I bought an option on a deal while my lawyer, Eddie Breger, was in the office. I told him he could get in on the deal for $3,000. Eddie said he'd like to, but right then he didn't have $3,000. The next day I sold the deal at a profit and gave him his share. Eddie said, 'But I never gave you the money.' I told him that it didn't matter so long as he had dealt himself in."

Hill was at the top rung of operators, with resources that more grandiose developers did not always command. He recalls getting a Saturday morning telephone call in the early 1960s from William Zeckendorf, then the highest-profile developer of all. "Back then, we kept office hours on Saturday morning," says Hill. "Zeckendorf asked me to come over to his office on East 47th Street. It was a couple of blocks from my office. Very fancy. Bill told me that he had a big deal for me in New Jersey. He was going to triple the money. All I needed to do was lend him $200,000. I asked him what part of the deal was mine. None, he said. But I'd get interest on the loan.

"I said, 'Bill, you made me walk over here to ask for a loan? Why didn't you come to my office? That's what people generally do when they want to borrow money.' We were sitting in his conference room, which had no windows. Bill felt that he was all the view anyone needed." (Hill does not say if he made the loan, but Zeckendorf's firm, Webb & Knapp, went bankrupt in 1965.)

Hill took possession of a major chunk of Manhattan history in 1954 when he bought a package of 60 properties on Third Avenue above and below 14th Street, originally part of a farm bought by Peter Stuyvesant in 1651. The property was sold by the estate of the Dutch governor's descendants. Over the next few years, Hill resold all the parcels.

As an operator, Hill bought and sold properties rapidly. He was less comfortable with assemblage, since that required a long-term outlook with no assurance of payback. Assemblage was typically done by those who could wait years to gain dominion over a site and sometimes hold off years more until the time was right to build on it. Seymour Durst, for example, spent decades assembling property along 42nd Street west of the Avenue of the Americas. His son, Douglas, finally announced construction of an office tower for the site beginning in 2004, almost 10 years after his father's death.

A conversation reported by Fred Hill suggests the unease felt by Ellen Hill, his mother and coinvestor in the Third Avenue assemblage. It took place at the Fontainbleu Hotel in Miami Beach, where Mrs. Hill was having afternoon coffee with a New York broker named William Ryan.

"Does my son know what he's doing, buying up all those properties on Third Avenue when he doesn't know if he can find a buyer?" asked the worried Ellen Hill, as her son told it.

"Mrs. Hill, at that site, you're sitting on diamonds," said Ryan.

"Maybe so," Ellen Hill answered, "but my rear end is getting really sore."

Her son may also have been getting a sore rear end from sitting on the assemblage, which could explain why he was willing to sell an option on the 52nd Street corner to Julien. Unlike Hill, Julien moved daily in the world of office building developers. If a buyer for the blockfront was out there, Julien was well positioned to find him. If the search came up cold after 90 days, Hill had informally offered Julien the right to extend the option for 90 days upon payment of an additional $25,000.

Asked about the price of the two buildings if he exercised his right of purchase, Julien professed not to remember, even though his memory for numbers is normally pinpoint. Perhaps that is because, whatever the price, he admits that he "certainly did not have the money to pay for the property." The gamble was that, before time ran out, Jullien could "flip" the contract to a developer with resources far larger than his own. Fred Hill could then also sell his five properties on the block to complete the assemblage.

In Julien's favor, the 52nd Street site was a prime example of "location, location, and location." Only two blocks to the west was Park Avenue's Seagram Building, already a classic.

One more block to the west stood 666 Fifth Avenue, the aluminum-clad headquarters of Tishman Realty & Construction Company, controlled by the city's best-known realty family. The site's proximity to mass transit was also critical in Julien's eyes. "The E train subway stop was right there," he says, "and the Lexington Avenue subway was at 51st Street."

With all that, the gamble that Julien took was still exactly that. In 1963, Julien's firm was nine years old and neither it nor he had deep pockets. "In those days, $25,000 was a lot of money," says Mike Solomon, who had been with the firm from its second year. "Julien's position was scary." It became scarier when he failed to find a purchaser for the blockfront in the first 90 days and lost his money to Fred Hill. "I was out of cash," says Julien, "and feeling kind of disgusted with myself for throwing so much money away." That sum would have bought a dozen new American Fords, Chevrolets, or Plymouths. Or a decent house in much of America.

Julien's lawyer, Barry Traub of Brooklyn-based Dreyer & Traub, lent Julien the next $25,000 to extend the option 90 more days. "The extension right was not in writing," says Traub, "but true to his word, Fred agreed to it. Julien was looking everywhere for a buyer and it looked like he had lost my $25,000. Then on the 89th day, I got a call from Julien. He said that if I could get over to 666 Fifth Avenue right away, we could make a deal. Tishman was ready to exercise the option at a small profit to us. We spent all day at their office and got the deal done."

Oddly, Julien remembers that Traub negotiated with Tishman while wearing a crewneck sweater. Normally, a lawyer of that era wore a suit. Traub's informality might not have suited another client. But it was in tune with informal aspects of Julien's business practice, such as that Ping-Pong table in his firm's Madison Avenue waiting room. Although Traub does not recall his casual wear that day, he does remember another sartorial detail connected to the Tishman deal. "Out of a sense that it was unfair that I made only a small profit on the sale of the option from Fred Hill," says Traub, "Julien gave me and my wife matching sealskin parkas."

Tishman, which was busy building in other cities but had not built an office tower in Manhattan since completing 666 Fifth Avenue in 1958, was now ready to be active on its home turf. Robert Tishman, president of the firm, negotiated to buy Julien's option on the two corner properties as well as the five owned by Hill. The developer now owned the entire blockfront between 52nd and 53rd Streets. Julien's profit on the sale of his option—in which Traub now participated—was modest. "What I really wanted," he says, "was an interest in the building. So I asked for it. If you don't ask, you don't get."

What Julien asked for from Tishman, he got: a 5 percent share in 866 Third Avenue, the 31-floor, 475,000-square-foot office building erected on the site. Designed by Emory Roth & Sons in standard curtain wall style, it was completed in 1966. Julien also asked for—and got—the right for his firm to be the rental agent for the new building. "With the help of other brokers, we rented it up," says Julien. One could read about it in the Studley Report, the firm's fledgling survey of office leasing.

Decades later, Julien used the "if you don't ask, you don't get" technique to address a particular concern of client, Cravath, Swaine & Moore. The law firm was negotiating the move from its seminal digs in Lower Manhattan up to Worldwide Plaza, the enormous, 24-elevator tower being built by William Zeckendorf Jr. (the next generation) on Eighth Avenue at 50th Street. "The rent was starting out cheap because Cravath was opening up new office territory," says Julien, "but it was going to escalate over time. In the discussion with the senior partners, they kept saying to me, 'We hope our younger partners don't find this to be a burden in later years.' It impressed me enormously that they weren't thinking only of themselves. So I said, 'Why don't we see if we can get you a piece of the building.' That way, the young partners would share in the revenue from escalation. I went back to Zeckendorf and said, 'Bill, we're ready to close a deal bringing you Cravath, but we want a piece of the building.'"

Julien secured an option for Cravath to purchase a share in Worldwide Plaza. But in the downturn of the early 1990s, the junior Zeckendorf "got in trouble" with the property and had to sell it to Blackstone Partners, a firm specializing in bottom fishing for distressed property. Cravath was induced by Blackstone to give up its option in order for the purchase to be consummated.

Tishman's purchase of the Third Avenue blockfront and plans to erect "a major office building" was reported in a five-paragraph article in the *New York Times* on February 4, 1964.

"Julien J. Studley, Inc., consultant to the Tishman interests in the transaction, has been named rental agent for the building," said the story. The partnership with the city's grandest developer was a milestone for Julien's still-young firm, putting it into the ranks of commercial brokerages with lengthier pedigrees. As 866 Third Avenue went up, Studley sponsored a student art show using the construction fence around the site as a gallery, giving the firm even more visibility.

As the building was being rented, Julien was called to Bob Tishman's office at 666 Fifth Avenue. "Bob said it was time to settle up the finances of my share in the building," says Julien. "I thought I'd have to put some more money up." Instead, Tishman handed him an envelope containing a check for $250,000.

"I don't understand," said Julien.

"We overmortgaged the building by $5 million," said Tishman. "Your 5 percent share comes to $250,000."

Overmortgaging was a little-known windfall that developers could reap. An office tower like 866 Third Avenue, for example, might have been built at a cost of $50 million and paid for with a construction loan in that amount. Once the tower was completed and as tenants began signing leases, the developer would convert the construction loan into a permanent mortgage. If the lender was willing to provide a sum larger than the cost of construction, so much the better. That surplus went directly into the pocket of the owner. Even though the owner had use of the funds, they were still owed to the lender. So they were treated as debt, not profit. Debt service is paid from revenues generated by rents and the interest portion is tax-deductible.

In 1972, Julien remembers getting an unexpected call from Bob Tishman. 866 Third Avenue, then six years old, was being sold. To postpone taxes, Julien needed to make a new purchase of property, within a year. That was known as a "tax swap." Tishman had one ready: A share in a new tower the developer was just completing at 919 Third Avenue, a few blocks north of the earlier tower. Designed by Skidmore Owings & Merrill, 919 was sleek and black, and at 1.4 million square feet, nearly triple the size of 866 Third Avenue. Julien's share was proportionately reduced to 1.75 percent.

A curiosity about 919 Third Avenue, and a reminder of the difficulty of midtown assemblages, was the lively, Lilliputian presence of P.J. Clarke's saloon and restaurant on the tower's plaza. Its owners had been loathe to sell out to Tishman, so an agreement was made in which they were given a 99-year lease on the site. But, in order for Tishman to qualify for a bonus of extra floors in his tower, P.J. Clarke's top two floors had to be lopped off to meet the height requirement for plaza structures.

"At 919 Third Avenue, we were active at leasing," says Julien. "We affiliated with a small brokerage firm which consolidated a group of carpet showrooms at 919. They wanted to be near the Decoration & Design Building at 979 Third. We got Tishman to set aside a block of 200,000 square feet for a carpet center. It was a good partnership, because we had the Tishman connection, and the other broker had the carpet connection."

Five years after getting a share in 919 Third Avenue, Julien got a call from young Jerry Speyer, Bob Tishman's partner, and just starting his ascent to the top of the real estate world. Jerry said they were liquidating Tishman Realty

& Development as a public company," says Julien. "One of the buildings being sold was 919." If Julien was to avoid exposure to tax payments on his profit so far, he would once more have to find a tax swap.

Two hundred and fifty thousand dollars would not go far in midtown Manhattan. But it was still real money in the outer boroughs. 'So now," Julien says, "I bought the pair of apartment buildings at 2899 and 2907 Kingsbridge Terrace in the Bronx. Two older, very classy guys were tired of owning and operating them." Both clad in utilitarian tan brick, the apartment buildings comprise 160 units. They were completed in the late 1920s by a developer who failed to attract tenants. A major problem was the lack of any nearby subway service. Unable to cope, the developer reportedly jumped to his death from the roof of one of the vacant buildings. A new owner is said to have succeeded in attracting renters by providing a shuttle bus to the subway station 10 blocks away.

Julien's purchase on Kingsbridge Terrace was not his first foray into the Bronx as a landlord. In the early 1970s, when the memory of the 1967 urban race riots kept away all but the most intrepid investors, he had bought an apartment house near Yankee Stadium. It had splendid Art Deco detailing and was called the Yankee Clipper. "Julien thought he was going to make a better world by being a caring landlord," said Gerry Freeman, his press-agent-cum-confidant. The tenants had other ideas. They went on a rent strike and Julien was forced to give up the building. "I delegated too much management authority, and I found out there were some nuts in the building who only wanted to be negative," says Julien. "That was my first taste of total failure."

Julien also had a rocky start as a landlord on Kingsbridge Terrace. The previous owners had been good managers. After their departure, a new managing agent failed to adequately screen tenants or maintain the buildings. Rents went unpaid. "I asked those two fellows to return for however long it took to get the buildings back on the old footing and we would split any profits," says Julien. "They did that and they also trained our current managing agent, Tom Webler." The tenant mix now includes so-called "Section 8" tenants, whose rents are subsidized or entirely covered by the Federal government. In New York, Section 8 applicants often come directly from homeless shelters. Some landlords are loathe to rent to them. But Webler interviews carefully. The entrance courtyards of each building are carefully tended by resident volunteers who have green thumbs: Mamie Walton at No. 2899 and Sylvia Lightbourne at No. 2907. The landscaping includes several varieties of azaleas, rhododendron, and roses, including rose of Sharon. "We give each of these ladies a couple of hundred dollars a year to cover the cost of plantings," said Webler, "and they do the rest."

When there is a problem at the buildings, Webler can be resourceful. for a time, for example, certain tenants were "airmailing" garbage from the west-facing windows. It landed on the roofs or yards of the private homes below. Webler got permission from one of the afflicted homeowners to install a surveillance camera looking up. He also painted the apartment number under each window. That way, when garbage was tossed out, the source could be identified precisely. The airmailing problem soon ended.

The Kingsbridge Terrace buildings might not look like most people's idea of a healthy real estate investment. Even by the time of Julien's purchase in 1978, the Bronx itself was still off-limits to many investors. The borough was then littered with abandoned residential buildings. Entire blocks of them, their windows boarded up, were plainly visible to drivers on the Cross Bronx Expressway. But better times slowly came back to the Bronx. At Julien's pair of buildings, patient nurturing paid off on the bottom line. Opening up the buildings' books, which he keeps for Julien, Stan Kovak said, "You'll see how the numbers pick up."

The records start with Julien's purchase of the two buildings for $700,000. The sellers took back a purchase money mortgage of $600,000, reducing Julien's cash investment to $100,000. By 1990, that mortgage had been paid off and the property refinanced several times. That year, he took out a $2.5 million mortgage—exactly 100 times the size of his option gamble with Fred Hill and the progenitor of the string of investments to come.

Bronx property values continued to rise through the 1990s, as families who had deserted the borough after World War II were replaced by an international cast of new immigrants. In 2000, Julien paid off the existing $2 million mortgage on the two buildings and took out a new $3.27 million mortgage. "The lender was Community Preservation Corporation," says Stan Kovak. "This government-supported institution encouraged you to make improvements by not requiring interest payments until the work was done. We put in new boilers, four new elevators, did façade and roof work. The interest rate on that loan was 7.67 percent."

In 2003, interest rates were dropping as Bronx property values rose. "It was a perfect market to either sell or refinance," says Kovak. Julien elected to once again refinance, this time through the Independence Savings Bank. The loan closed in early 2004. "We got a $4.5 million mortgage commitment on the two buildings," says Kovak. "The interest was 2 percent less: 5.67 percent on the new loan compared to 7.67 percent on the old one. There are a few costs that Julien bore, mainly a penalty for paying off the old mortgage. That's called a yield maintenance charge and it came to about $100,000. Still, even though the new loan is bigger, it costs about the same to carry as the old smaller loan.

"The real story of Julien's investment," says Kovak, "is that, if the property is good, every few years you'll be able to take money out through refinancing. Julien had about $2.8 million in debt to pay off on the old loan. Now the bank lends him $4.5 million, meaning that roughly $1.5 million comes to him. The difference between what you are paying off and what you are getting is tax-free. It's one of the unseen reasons why people do real estate." Julien points out, however, that the reason he was able to take out that $1.5 million is because interest rates went down steadily: "Lower interest costs are more important than any rise in the value of the property."

Julien has been conservative in financing his Kingsbridge Terrace buildings. They are valued by investors and lenders at about six times their annual rental income, also called the "rent roll." The properties bring in $1.1 million annually, making their value $6.6 million. Since banks will lend up to 80 percent of the property value, Julien's mortgage could have been as high as $5.2 million, rather than the $4.5 million loan that he actually took. "I don't want to put the buildings under strain," says Julien. "I want to keep high cash flow so that there will be ample reserves in case we have to do major repairs."

While the elevators were being replaced in the two buildings in 1996, Julien decided it would be nice to do something for the tenants who were being forced to walk up the stairs. Just before Thanksgiving that year, every tenant received a turkey. At Christmas, it was a ham. Now the gifts are an annual tradition. "When tenants from other buildings learn about what we do," says Terrance Ram, superintendent of No. 2309, "they say 'You're getting hams? And turkeys?' Their eyes are wide." Rather than make tenants do their own pick-up, Terrance loads up a shopping cart with the hams and turkeys and personally makes door-to-door deliveries. "Mostly, tenants see me when they need something fixed," says Ram. "This moment is about good feelings."

Forty years after the Tishman deal, 88-year-old Fred Hill was still "operating" from a former townhouse at 14 East 52nd Street. The forked tail of an enormous blue marlin arches over the doorway of Hill's second floor office. Another stuffed marlin, this one an entire eight-footer, dominates an interior wall. A myriad of trophies attest to his skills as a big game angler.

Hill was carrying two wrapped bouquets of fresh flowers when he bustled into his office, a few minutes late for an interview on a Friday morning. With the help of an assistant, he arranged the flowers in vases before sitting down at his desk. Julien remembers that Hill was a redhead when they did their deal, but now Hill's thatch of hair is white.

Before our interview began, Hill took a call from his stock broker and, after close questioning, ordered gold futures, Then he talked with one of his daughters. Finally, he swiveled his chair toward my way and fixed me with his clear blue eyes.

"Would you know that I'm legally blind?" he asked.

"Not at all. Can you see the pattern on my tie?"

"Not so well. I can see your eyeglasses,"

"Well then," I asked, "can you see the flowers that you put in the two vases over in the corner?"

"No," said Hill.

"So why do you buy them if you can't see them?"

"They're not for me. They're for my lady."

And then Hill unexpectedly told a story: "When I was about 19, I fell in love with a girl named Sylvia Whyte. But my parents thought she had no brains and they forced me to break it off. They were wrong about Sylvia. She became a successful designer of children's clothes. Maybe the very best designer of all. Meanwhile, I married someone else and we had two daughters. Several years ago, my wife died. I thought Sylvia Whyte might be in Florida. Information gave me a listing in that name."

Hill dialed a number he got from information and a woman's voice answered. "This is Fred Hill," he said. "Is this the Sylvia Whyte whom I wanted to marry 66 years ago?"

"Yes," she answered.

As Hill was a widower, Whyte was a widow. They talked easily. Hill invited her to New York. They lunched with his daughters at La Grenouille, the classic French restaurant opposite his office. Hill was then about to go on vacation in Mexico with his daughters. "They said to me, why don't you invite Sylvia to come along as our guest?" Hill took their advice, and Whyte agreed to the idea. She and Hill have been together ever since. "On Fridays, I buy her flowers," he said, glancing in the direction of the vases he could not see.

Unlike Hill, lawyer Barry Traub bowed out of the New York real estate arena soon after representing Julien in the 866 Third Avenue deal and moved to Marin County near San Francisco. He invested in real estate and publishing, but never again practiced law. "In his offhand way of offering advice," says Traub, "Julien was responsible for giving me two necessary insights into my new life." One came when Julien visited Traub and his wife at their new home in a woodsy setting with a view of Mount Tamalpais. "'Barry,' Julien said to me, 'This is really beautiful... *if* you like beauty.' What he meant was that I shouldn't forget that my wife and I were from Brooklyn. We are city kids!"

Traub's other insight was delivered following a poker game in Manhattan. It was nearly the eve of Traub's departure for California. "I told Julien that I wanted to put together a group to buy a building in San Francisco," says Traub. "But I couldn't even get the owner to speak to me. I was ready to give up. Julien asked me if I was planning to practice law in California. When I answered no, he said, 'Now that you are no longer a lawyer, you need to understand that when somebody tells you no, that's when you get started.' "

Traub took Julien's advice and got his building. Julien's way with Traub was not so different from how he handled the brokers at his firm. "He was like a mother hen," says Traub, "picking them up when they were down, putting them down when they were too far up. They all needed a certain kind of cuddling that he knew how to give them."

Julien has done a number of property investment deals since the first one that began on Third Avenue. All have been highly profitable. But, says Julien, "I can think of two deals which gave me more than profits."

By far the bigger of the two was the $193 million metamorphosis of the stately but outmoded post office next to Union Station in Washington, D.C. Designed in monumental Beaux Arts style by Graham and Burnham in 1911, the granite-columned building then boasted the ultimate in automated mail handling equipment. By 1986, its functions had been shifted to a new facility.

"One morning in 1985," says Julien, "I saw a notice in the newspaper announcing a competition for bids on redeveloping the post office. It was to be called Postal Square and the postal service would still own it. But a 30-year master lease would be awarded to the winning bidder. That would be whoever offered the most base rent to the postal service as well as a participation in any profits. It was up to the bidders to figure out the usage. There were only two restrictions: The ground floor lobby had to become a postal museum and the landmarked façade had to be restored."

Studley's proposal to create a government center with almost 900,000 square feet of office space won the bidding. The firm partnered first with Arthur Cohen, a New York developer, and the giant Hines Interests Limited Partnership. "The building had vast 160,000-square-foot floor plates," says Julien. "That meant not enough windows for private tenants like law firms. But big floors could suit certain big government agencies." The U.S. General Services Administration agreed. It leased the entire building for 30 years and installed the Bureau of Labor Statistics in 620,000 square feet and the U.S. Senate Services Center in 170,000 square feet. The street-level National Postal Museum got 70,000 square feet in a painstakingly restored lobby home.

Julien wondered why, since the post office was to be converted to federal offices, the government itself had not redeveloped the building. "I was told no agency would believe the bureaucrats who promised move-in by a certain date. So they would refuse to sign a lease. But they would have faith in a commercial developer that the space would be ready on schedule."

New office space totaling 450,000 square feet was cleverly added to the rear of Postal Square after a plan to add three extra floors was rejected by preservationists. That additional space made the project financially viable. But the rescue of the formal lobby was purely a labor of love. In a 1957 modernization, the grand space was mostly stripped of its superbly crafted and varied original details. Among the missing, as reported in *Building Design & Construction* (October 1993), were 26 marble screens and consoles, a marble cornice, stone writing tables, pilasters and grills, 24 carved marble lighting torchieres, and all but seven of the ceiling's original plaster coffers. Restoration and replication did much to bring back Graham and Burnham's grand vision—within limits. Although cost ruled out recreating the original torchieres carved from Carrara marble, for example, replicas were cast from bronze, bringing a new warmth to the lobby. And missing plaster ceiling coffers were remolded from glass fiber–reinforced gypsum. A false ceiling, installed in 1957 to create an additional floor, was removed, bringing back the original generous dimensions of the hall.

"One of our proudest moments as a firm," says Julien, "was the grand opening of that wonderful space. It had been dead and now it was alive with people. All kinds of groups started using it for parties."

The other investment deal that gave Julien "more than profits" was far smaller than Postal Square. It was the purchase of a small commercial building at 18 East 42nd Street, between Fifth and Madison Avenues. The building was only 25 feet wide, but ownership included a plot of land under an adjacent building which fronted on Fifth Avenue. "This happened in 1982," says Julien, "and I had a new assistant working for me named Marion Kennedy. She was loyal, but more than that, she was exceptionally helpful in whatever needed to be done. She had no experience in real estate, and I thought it would be nice to give her a flavor of what it was all about. So I gave her a one percent share in 18 East 42nd Street."

The next year, Kennedy left Studley to have the first of her two children. Sixteen years passed in which Julien had no contact with his former assistant and silent partner in the property. Then, in 1999, 18 East 42nd Street was sold as part of an assemblage for a new office tower. "I had to find Marion so that she could get her share," says Julien. Kennedy, who lived on Long Island, did not return the first several calls from Studley. "I thought that the only reason they'd contact me was for a cash call on the building," she says."Like maybe I was supposed to chip in to pay for a new roof or boiler."

When he did finally reach Kennedy, Julien informed her that she was in line to get, not give, cash at 18 East 42nd Street. And he had a question: Now that her children were no longer small, was she interested in returning to work as his assistant? Kennedy was soon back at her desk beside Julien's office."Getting her back," says Julien,"was the big bonus in that deal."

11 People Broker

"I don't see that it's a main point of my life to find faults in other people"

—Julien Studley

"Come walk over to the bank with me," said Julien, striding out of his office. "You can be my body guard."

It was the afternoon before he was to drive with his wife Jane to the vast Foxwoods casino in Connecticut for a poker tournament. On this crisp autumn day, we strolled three blocks down Park Avenue to Julien's Chase banking branch. A young bank officer named Flavio was expecting us. Checking around first to see that nobody was within earshot—at 3:15 P.M. the bank was not crowded—Flavio whispered, "So you want $20,000 in cash plus a cashier's check for $20,000. Is that right Mr. Studley?"

Julien nodded.

"And this gentleman with you is....

"My bodyguard."

"Excellent. Please come with me and Rosie will take care of you at the cashier's window."

Rosie quickly cut the cashier's check. But she did not have $20,000 in her cash drawer. She excused herself for several minutes before returning with two hefty packets of bills with which she plumped up a manila envelope. Then she began filling out U.S. Treasury Form 4789, a currency transaction report required for all cash withdrawals or deposits over $10,000.

"What is your profession?" asked Rosie.

"Executive."

Rosie looked up quizzically through the window bars. "I don't believe that's specific enough, Mr. Studley."

"Well, my title is founding chairman," said Julien, warming up to a bit of gamesmanship with Rosie.

"Founding chairman..." Rosie pondered for a slow moment before shaking her head. "I'm afraid that the government won't go for that, either. Does founding chairman mean that you're retired? They'll accept 'retired.'"

Julien drew back, his eyes widening, as if the "r word" couldn't possibly be applied to a man over the age of 75.

"Oh, but I'm not retired," he said. "I've just come from my office."

Rosie drummed her ballpoint pen. "I'd better check with my supervisor," she said. Soon, a tall man with a neatly trimmed beard arrived. "Mr. Studley," he said with an air of authority, "Don't you own a real estate firm?"

"I've sold my interest. But I am the founding chairman and I still go every day to my office."

"So you're a real estate broker then..."

"I am a broker," said Julien, without enthusiasm, "but I was never a very good one." The banker raised his eyebrows.

"Let's put that down anyway, Mr. Studley."

Julien nodded. The negotiation, which in its probe and parry seemed like a warm-up for the poker tournament, was over.

Strolling back to the office, Julien said, "It's true that I was never a very good broker. After about my second year in the business, it wasn't my main role. I was better at guiding the business. Now that I'm no longer running the show, I am more of a broker of people."

As practiced by Julien, people brokering means more than putting individuals together and hoping for synergy. It also means supplying the voltage of an idea that the concerned parties can grab hold of—one that they might not expect. Don Schnabel once said, trying to define the broker's role, "The Rockefellers thought they were in the oil business, when it was actually energy. The Vanderbilts thought they were in railroads, when it was really transportation. Brokers think they are selling space, when they're actually trying to make connections between tenants and landlords." At Studley, Julien constantly "flipped the switch" connecting brokers and clients. No longer the leader of his firm, he is still a broker of people. Now he does it as a trustee or board member of several public institutions. They include the New School, the Graduate Center of City University Foundation, Palladia (formerly Project Return), Lincoln Center for the Performing Arts, and the Film Society of Lincoln Center.

Julien's input is not always welcomed. "The tendency of people who get asked to serve on institutional boards is to be rather passive," he says. "They get in line with what management wants to do. But the whole point of board oversight is to cast a dispassionate eye on what salaried management is doing. It's never easy to call attention to wrong directions, because as a trustee you naturally want to be cozy with the career people."

Calling attention to new directions is what comes most naturally to Julien. Strolling back to his office from the bank, the money envelope tucked in the pocket of his London-tailored sports jacket, Julien told me about his front-burner project for the New School, where he is a trustee and vice chairman. The previous Saturday evening, he'd hosted a dinner at Honmura An, a Japanese restaurant on Mercer Street in Soho known for its stylish clientele and its soba noodles, homemade from special buckwheat flour. Julien's guests were Bob Kerrey, president of the New School, and Jim Murtha, the school's executive vice president.

"Jane and I often go to Hanmura An after we've driven home from the country on Sunday evening," said Julien. "Jane says that's the only time that she doesn't feel like cooking dinner. It's not the greatest food in New York, though it is the most reliable. But I had a particular reason for bringing Bob and Jim there."

"To taste the soba noodles?" I asked

"No," said Julien. "To see the flowers." And then he backtracked. Way back.

Ten years earlier, Julien had brokered the sale to the New School of a medium-sized midblock commercial building at 55 West 13th Street now called University Hall. "Even further back, a design store called Bon Marché had been on the ground floor," says Julien. "Some space and the loading dock were occupied by other tenants, but the building was mainly vacant. It was a very good buy—only about $3 million." When the last of the holdover leases expired in 2002, an airy lobby was created on 13th Street and much of the second floor was converted into a large lecture hall with advanced audiovisual features. The remainder of the floor became a reception suite, including dining facilities, for New School officials and guests. The suite was named in memory of Dorothy Hirshon, who had served the school as a trustee for 61 years.

Julien sat next to Kerrey at the dinner inaugurating the Hirshon Suite."I noticed that the walls seemed awfully bare," he says. Bare enough so that Randolph Swearer, the dean of the university's Parsons School of Design, was able to use one as a projection screen for his presentation. "I leaned over to Bob and suggested that we do something about those walls," says Julien.

"You're in charge," replied Kerrey. He suggested that Swearer be consulted on what might be done. Julien felt that a design solution for the trustees' room need not be as conventional as hanging framed pictures on the walls. "Swearer asked for some time to think about that," says Julien. "When he called back, he put me in touch with Brian Tolle."

A Brooklyn-born sculptor and part-time Parsons instructor, Tolle had designed the ambitious Irish Hunger Memorial on a broad lawn at Battery Park City, two blocks north of Ground Zero. A not-so-little slice of the "auld sod," the memorial includes a stone wall, cottage, and even earth shipped from Ireland. In a quite different project commissioned by the city of Ghent, Belgium, Tolle had gone high-tech. Selecting a sixteenth century building facing a canal, the artist used three-dimensional digital imagery to simulate what a reflection of the façade would look like after being disturbed by the wake of a passing boat. Using the digital files, a New Jersey foundry created a full-scale metal version of the undulant reflection. Shipped to Ghent, it was installed in front of the original building on the canal so that a viewer could contemplate both the real and reflected façades.

Julien had read about the Ghent project before meeting Tolle. "When I talked to Brian, he asked if I wanted something of that kind for the trustees' suite, or did I want something with moving parts—not mobile in a mechanical way, but in a video sense. I told him I didn't know what I wanted." Just as Kerrey had put no restrictions on Julien in developing a plan for the suite, Julien was putting none on Tolle. "I felt that whatever Brian might do could generate buzz for the New School," he says.

Tolle agreed to work on a proposal for the project jointly with Parsons' digital design department. His fee of $10,000 was to be covered by Julien. "We're going far beyond what we'd first imagined," Julien told Kerrey after meeting with Tolle. That was fine with Kerrey. "I am willing to wager that we will all be impressed by what Brian will propose. If not, we will have had the chance to assess some interesting ideas," Julien wrote in a memo to other board members. Meanwhile, as the Tolle commission was being developed, the walls of the Hirshon Suite were no longer bare. A New School art advisory panel had hung them with prints by Robert Rauschenberg, incorporating old newspaper clippings about labor strife, Mafia hits, and other gritty urban doings. "The prints were nice," says Julien, "but the room was still a bit lugubrious. I thought that, for the time being, we could lighten it up with flowers. That's when Honmura An popped into my mind."

In earlier years, Julien describes the floral arrangements at the restaurant as having been "very Zen, even bare in feeling." But the mood changed with the arrival in 2003 of a new, young maître d' named Katsuya Nishimori, known as Katsu. "This fellow made his own striking arrangements of flowers, branches, and vines," says Julien. "Their mode was more architectural than floral, and much different from what you'd see in a French restaurant—spare rather than opulent. Katsu and Jane would exchange comments about what he'd done. I thought Katsu's touch would help out our space on West 13th Street. And that's why I took Bob Kerrey and Jim Murtha to the Honmura An—to see how they liked the flowers."

They agreed that the Hirshon Suite could do with a bit of Nishimori's flair. Julien's instinct for discovering talent was on point. Nishimori, it turned out, had a "day job" as manager of the floral boutique of Takashimaya, the Japanese department store on Fifth Avenue. In style and clientele, Takashimaya is a kind of retail alter ego to Honmura An. Nishimori, trained as a chemist and then as an artist in his native Japan, had been hired by the store to give a more distinctive look to the flower boutique, which has pride of place at the front of the store. Pedestrians on Fifth Avenue can see into it. Soon after taking over, Nishimori took advantage of the boutique's soaring ceiling by suspending giant, billowy spirals of bleached willow shoots overhead, stringing them with rings of birch bark. Stolid agave and yucca fronds interacted with delicate masses of lilies. A long stem of crimson ginger flower seemed to grow out of the hollow of a bamboo cane. Nishimori brought the look of Takashimaya to Honmura An.

Julien invited Nishimori to visit the New School. Their first stop was the school's original building at 46 West 12th Street, where they saw six renowned frescoes on revolutionary themes, each 40 feet long, created in 1931 for the new building by José Clemente Orozco. Next, the two men walked around the corner to University Center. Its new double-height lobby features a mural donated by Sol LeWitt. Upstairs, they saw the Hirshon Suite. Nishimori agreed to provide a weekly floral arrangement designed for the space. The $250 weekly bill is sent to Julien. The first arrangement, delivered in November 2003 and set in a tall, rectangular, iron red ceramic vase, featured large lilies in dark and pale shades of red, accented by long spikes of palm.

Julien's rapport with Bob Kerrey—and his people brokering—goes back to 1999 when Julien attended a Congressional hearing in Washington as a member of the CEO Forum on Education and Technology. The group's purpose was to push for technological literacy in America's classrooms. Kerrey, a Vietnam veteran who had been awarded the Congressional Medal of Honor, was then in his second term as a Democratic Senator from Nebraska. "Bob said that in his state there was a problem with minority students learning math," says Julien. "He wanted to know if our group had addressed that problem. We didn't have an answer so the question wasn't appreciated by everyone. But I liked Bob's forthrightness. I told a friend who knows everyone in Washington that I'd like to meet Bob. And then I got a call from him. He said, 'I heard you wanted to meet me.' And he wasn't even looking for a campaign contribution."

Julien did more than meet Kerrey. He suggested to the New School, then seeking a new president, that Kerrey was the right person for the job. The senator had been gearing up to seek a third term. Instead, in February 2001, he became the seventh president of New School University. The school's first president, when it was called the New School for Social Research, had been Alvin Johnson, also a Nebraskan. That same winter, Kerrey married Sarah Paley, a New York screen writer who had once worked for "Saturday Night Live." Their son, Henry, was born on September 10, 2001.

In April 2002, a long-ago horrific night in Vietnam resurfaced to haunt Kerrey. As reported in *New York Times Magazine* in spring, 2001, at least a dozen civilians had been killed by American fire on that night in February 1969 in a village called Thanh Phong, which was thought to be filled with Viet Cong. The élite navy seal unit that did the killing was commanded by 25-year-old Bob Kerrey. It remains unclear why civilians were killed that night. But when the *Times* story was published, Julien was clear about one thing: Kerrey should have alerted him to what had happened as a precondition to the New School nomination. Indeed, some in the press had already discussed the events of that night with Kerrey. Julien slept poorly for many nights. "I felt responsible to the New School for the situation," he says.

Julien invited Kerrey to a lunch at which "we had it out and cleared the air." The bond between the two men was once again tight.

Despite their widely different backgrounds, Julien and Kerrey share some offbeat core values. For both, their allegiance to America eminates far from the standard rhetoric of patriotism. In Kerrey's case, that became clear as he questioned US Attorney General John Ashcroft during a hearing, on April 13, 2004, of the presidential panel investigating intelligence failures before 9/11. "I wasn't in the Congress when the Patriot Act passed, and you know me well enough (both men served together as senators) that anything you have to put the word "patriot" on in order to get people to vote for it, I'm inclined to vote against it just on that basis."

"I do know you," said Ashcroft.

That exchange reminded me of an evening in a Buenos Aeries restaurant during the 2001 winter trip. Back home, the Superbowl was about to begin, and a big screen television had been brought into the restaurant so that the brokers could watch. All rose and bellowed out the National Anthem. All except Julien. One might say that he was voting against too-easy patriotism. Had Kerrey been on hand, he probably would have sat out the anthem with Julien.

In January 2004, Kerrey invited Julien to be his guest at the annual Alfalfa Club dinner at the Washington Hilton—and, as it turned out, gave him a chance to do a brief bit of people brokering. "I didn't even know until an hour before leaving New York that this event was black tie," says Julien. "And I didn't know anything about the Alfalfa Club. But when I entered the hotel lobby, I started to see four-star generals and all the Bush family." Julien noticed that among his tablemates was Henry Kissinger. "Sitting on the other side of me from Bob was Jim Lehrer of public television," says Julien. "I learned from Lehrer that he and Bob had not been talking since the three televised debates between Gore and Bush in 2000. Bob publicly criticized Lehrer for not having moderated the debates fairly, and that offended Lehrer. I said to Bob, 'You're a good man. Jim is a good man. So why keep up a feud?' Bob said, 'You're right.' He apologized to Jim and as of the Alfalfa dinner they are talking again."

Sometimes the art and practice of people brokering is about repairing damage done by others. A good deal of that had been done by Lincoln Center to the 120-year-old Good Shepherd–Faith Presbyterian Church, at 152 West 66th Street. Or so the congregants felt. The stolid, tan-brick church is the only surviving building from an earlier era on the three-square-block culture campus, completed in 1968. As a board member of both Lincoln Center and the Film Society of Lincoln Center, where he is also chair of the executive committee, Julien was called upon to repair wounded relations with the church.

At one time, Good Shepherd-Faith was being eyed by Lincoln Center as a potential site for expansion. The Film Society's Walter Reade Theater, a mecca for film buffs, adjoins the church. "We weren't aggressive," says Julien, "But it was a time when Lincoln Center saw lots of money coming in, and management said, 'Hey, why don't you fantasize what you would like to have.' The Film Society thought it would be nice to add two small theaters." An architect drew up a plan for a nine story building on the church site in which Good Shepherd-

Faith would keep the ground floor plus two additional levels. The other six floors would be divided between Juilliard, The School of American Ballet, and the Film Society. "This wasn't going to be an office building taking over from the church," says Julien. "It would be an improved facility for the church, with Lincoln Center's space above."

Early approaches to the church by Lincoln Center operatives had been indelicate. An incident that particularly grated on the church elders was the unannounced arrival of a Lincoln Center executive who walked into the church office and announced that his institution was ready to purchase the church site. Learning that the minister could not see him, the executive left his card and disappeared. That approach, in the eyes of church elder John Gingrich, was an indicator of a powerful institution's attitude toward a struggling church of diverse ethnicity. "You have to understand that the way they built Lincoln Center, the welcome mat is out on the Broadway side and the cold shoulder is to the Amsterdam Avenue side, where the housing projects are," says Gingrich. "It's a class thing."

Enter Julien. On behalf of both Lincoln Center and the Film Society, he invited Gingrich to lunch, at which he learned about "the element of condescension" the church felt emanating from its powerful neighbor. Julien was sympathetic but firm. When Gingrich referred to the "unwholesome past," Julien says that he responded, "Look, I can't answer to the past." Next, Julien met with church congregants. "Our people were all ratcheted up," says Gingrich. "Their position toward Julien was, if you're here representing Lincoln Center, our feeling is negative."

Prior to that meeting, Julien sent a letter to church members invoking the example of Saint Peter's Lutheran Church, and Citibank (Chapter 5). Like Good Shepherd–Grace, Saint Peter's was an old church that had been overwhelmed by its surroundings—in this case, intense commercial development. Julien suggested that a scenario similar to that of Saint Peter's could perhaps benefit Good Shepherd–Grace and Lincoln Center, creating new space for both.

"This was the first presentation I'd made alone to the elders in the presence of the pastor," says Julien of that meeting. "Later, when we made some progress, I met with them again, this time bringing the presidents of Juilliard and the Film Society. They let us know how they felt about the past. The pastor was miffed at how she had been treated when Lincoln Center first wanted to buy the property. The African-American ladies were unhappy about how the public housing community to the west had been treated. They really made us squirm. But when they sensed we were open-minded, they softened. At the end, they gave us cookies and hugs."

Lacking funds, Lincoln Center did not pursue the church project. And yet, as Rebecca Robertson, the institution's Executive Director of Redevelopment, points out, something important had happened. "It had been a different con versation before," she says. "Julien really does struggle to understand how other people feel. And he was able to open a dialogue with the church that had been closed."

Lincoln Center backed away from its interest in the church. "As they looked at the price of a new building," says Julien, "interest shifted to creating additional space in property already owned by the institution on West 65th Street between Broadway and Amsterdam Avenue." On the south side of that dreary blockfront is Avery Fisher Hall. On the north side is Juilliard. What the church felt—that it was treated shabbily by the institution—is what West 65th Street would say of itself if a street could speak. Here, at the epicenter of American culture, 65th Street might as well be servicing an industrial zone. Both sides are pocked with loading bays and parking garage entrances. At midblock, the street is darkened by a pedestrian overpass, called Milstein Plaza, connecting the main performance halls south of 65th Street with the Juilliard School and the Walter Reade Theater to the north. From above, the walkway is pleasant. From underneath, it is dingy and dispiriting.

The travertine sheathing of the buildings lining West 65th Street, originally a creamy white, is grey and grimy. And yet, as Rebecca Robertson points out, this single block is where thousands of people work or study daily: a massing point of the arts. To belatedly figure out how to provide the kind of attractive street that all these talented people deserve, Lincoln Center formed the West 65th Street Working Group in the late 1990s. Back then, Julien and Bruce Kovner, chairman of Juilliard, briefed Mayor Rudolph Guiliani on the early planning for a new 65th Street. "The mayor was very attentive," says Julien. "He asked all the right questions."

The rethinking of West 65th Street has been entrusted to a team of architectural firms led by Diller Scofidio & Renfro. The partnership's projects range from the redesigned Brasserie in the Seagram Building, with its bank of televisions above the bar monitoring images of customers entering the restaurant, to the "blur building" hovering on Lake Neuchâtel during Swiss Expo 2003.

"Right now, you reach Juilliard and the Walter Reade Theater from above," says Julien. "The plan is to remove the balcony and make user-friendly theater and Juilliard School entrances with lots of glass at street level." Also slated to be removed is access to an underground parking garage used by Lincoln Center audiences on the south side of 65th Street. A new tunnel would be dug under the street connecting to an existing access point on 66th Street. Users would enter the garage by another access point around the corner on Amsterdam Avenue. One less amenity for cars would be one more amenity for walkers, but that aspect of the plan "provoked a big fight with the opera," according to Julien. "When opera patrons come in, they do it underground. So there is some worry that if they have one less entrance to the garage, there could be a jam-up at the one that remains."

During a meeting at which the West 65th Street Working Group was about to endorse the garage alteration, Julien says, "I asked the question nobody else wanted to ask: 'Is there anybody who may not be in this room right now who could say no to this project even though we all say yes?'" There was no doubt about who Julien had in mind. It was Joseph Volpe, who had risen from apprentice carpenter to general manager of the Met. Volpe was a pugnacious guardian of his institution's prerogatives, and he was not at the meeting of the working group. Julien shortly heard from him by telephone. "Joe said, 'I heard that you alluded to me.' He wasn't happy. But we smoothed it out. Joe actually said he felt a connection to me because we both came up from poor origins."

Julien is normally a peacemaker. But as a trustee, as when he led Studley, he also can occasionally erupt. It happened in the fall of 2002 when Peter Lehrer was named to head up the Lincoln Center Reconstruction Project. The task of the project is to put in motion a $1.2 billion makeover of the nearly 40-year-old Performing Arts Center, including the redesign of West 65th Street. Lehrer is co-founder of Lehrer McGovern, the enormous construction company now called Lehrer McGovern Bovis. Julien's anger at Lehrer's appointment had multiple flash points, starting with fact that, as he says, "Peter's function was not properly explained. He was supposed to be directing people without running things. That was Rebecca Robertson's role. But Peter is a hands-on guy, so you could guess that there would be conflict. Peter is also from the contracting world, and he is a master of that. But I felt the job was better suited to a developer. To be successful in New York, a developer needs political skills above all. That's not primary when you're a contractor. I was fuming when this appointment to head up a key committee that I am a member of was done without consulting me."

Julien's view seems to have been validated when Lehrer abruptly resigned as head of the reconstruction project in October, 2002, just a month after taking on the job. "A lot of money has been spent on planning without enough to show for it," Lehrer told the *New York Times*. The article reported that, as Julien had foreseen, Lehrer had "clashed" with Rebecca Robertson, and had demanded that she be replaced, an ultimatum that was rejected by Lincoln Center chairman Bruce Crawford.

"At a Lincoln Center board meeting after the resignation," says Julien, "A strange thing happened: both Rebecca and Peter were there, even though they were not board members. I stood up and said that it wasn't right to blame either of them for what happened. Lincoln Center's management was to blame, because it had set up the dynamic which led to Peter's resignation. Peter came up after the meeting and shook my hand. Rebecca had won the battle, but I tried to clean up the blood."

Not long after Lehrer's resignaton, Julien gave a luncheon for Dick Gephardt, congressman from Missouri and former House majority leader, who was starting his run for the 2004 Democratic Presidential nomination. "Though I had invited Peter,"says Julien, "I was surprised that he showed up, knowing that I had been against his appointment at Lincoln Center. But he also appreciated that I had not blamed him for how things turned out."

"I was glad to attend Julien's lunch," says Peter Lehrer, "because at the board meeting after I had resigned out of frustration, Julien was the only one who stood up and said, 'Look, we did not give Peter the authority to do the job we asked him to do.' Julien spoke with courage and a lot of insight."

At that tense board meeting, Lehrer says, "They said, 'We're going to discuss Peter's resignation and we think he should leave the room.' But nobody seconded the motion, so I sat there." In Julien's eyes, the presence of Lehrer and Robertson was also a management failure, "If we were going to discuss this situation,"explains Julien, "Then Peter and Rebecca should have been asked not to attend."

The new vision of West 65th Street as an "Avenue of the Arts" will be not be complete, in Julien's eyes, unless it finds ways to be hospitable to the students of Martin Luther King High School and La Guardia High School for the Performing

Arts. Both schools are on Amsterdam Avenue directly across from Lincoln Center. "Thousands of students use West 65th Street daily on their way to and from Broadway," says Julien. "But Lincoln Center has not found any meaningful way to connect with these kids."

In the autumn of 2003, Julien spotted an opportunity to create an institutional connection to the high schoolers at an unpromising spot: a littered stairway at 65th Street and Amsterdam Avenue leading up to the second level of Lincoln Center. "Management wanted to turn this space into a Lincoln Center gift shop," says Julien. "but it was wrong for retail because, basically, there's zero foot traffic except for students, and they're not going to be customers. Then it occurred to me—let's try to create a hangout there for the kids where they could sit and have a snack and listen to music. It would bring down the average age of people using Lincoln Center. That gave me another idea. I had just met a guy who is high up in the music business. I telephoned him and asked if he might be interested in sponsoring a music café for the kids who could come in after school. He was instantly hot for it."

Ten days had passed since Julien had gone to play poker at Foxwoods. It was hard not to notice, as he spoke excitedly about the café concept, that he had a black eye. Rising from his desk to greet me, he hobbled from bruised knees. Had Julien gotten into a poker brawl?

Not at all, he explained. His brother George had stayed for a few days with him and Jane at Foxwoods. Then Julien had driven George to New London, Connecticut, so that he could catch the train back to New York from the large old red brick station, survivor of an era when such stations were a focus of civic pride. "I'd never seen that building," said Julien. "It was impressive from the front, even more so from the platform side. I told George that it looked like it might have been designed in the 1880s by H.H. Richardson [1838–1886], who is maybe my favorite nineteenth century architect.

"I was looking up, trying to get a better view of the roof, which is inset with unusual windows, not watching where I was stepping. And I tripped over a cobblestone and fell down face first. I was a mess. George didn't want to leave me but I insisted that he catch his train. Then I bought some alcohol at the drug store and cleaned myself up. When I got back to Foxwoods, Jane took one look at me and she'd never let me out of her sight again."

Julien pointed to a book on his coffee table next to a vase full of white roses. It was a survey of H.H. Richardson's buildings. "I guessed right" Julien said. "The station is by Richardson. He designed it in 1885. That almost makes it worth falling down."

Not every man of Julien's age, or any age, would agree that nailing the provenance of a train station is worth a black eye and two swollen knees. But, as the business he built and the culture he nurtured suggest, Julien isn't Everyman.

Epilogue

Julien was cool to the title of this book. In his eyes, the city skyline has been shaped by actual builders rather than by brokers. Yet his firm's role was undeniable, and continued to be so in the spring of 2004, the second year of new leadership at Studley. In that season, the firm had a hand in two projects whose completion altered the Manhattan skyline in quite different ways.

One was Time Warner Center, whose paired, 750-foot-high towers soar seemingly without mass over Columbus Circle—a stealth skyscraper, if you will. Climaxing an eight-year-long run of work for Time Warner, Studley represented this client in the financing, planning, and construction cost eyeballing of its portion of the multi-use complex. The city's most important commercial building project in decades, the center incorporates office space anchored by Time Warner's corporate headquarters and CNN studios, a Mandarin Oriental hotel, shops including a giant Whole Foods supermarket, distinguished restaurants, Jazz at Lincoln Center, and high floor apartments.

Studley's role was familiar—fighting for the client. During the center's construction design phase, for example, Studley argued with the lead developer, Related Companies, that Time Warner was being inequitably charged for its scheduled share of the building's vertical steel support columns. The developer wanted Time Warner to pay for the proportional cost of the steelwork running through its space on floors 5 through 22. At first glance, this seemed fair. But Studley pointed out that the columns within Time Warner's space needed to be more massive, and therefore more expensive, than those above, because they had to support the entire 54-floor edifice. Owners of those upper floors, insisted Studley, should share in the cost of fabricating and installing the columns in Time Warner's space. A "matchstick" model of the building's skeleton was painstakingly constructed, each element color-coded to show its load. In the end, Studley won a reduction in its client's share of the steelwork cost. Studley's fee for the multi-front representation of Time Warner was the biggest in the firm's history.

The city's psychological skyline also changed in that spring of 2004. This was the result of a major law firm's decision to move from its self-owned building on Maiden Lane in Lower Manhattan to 450,000 square feet at One World Financial Center—the edge of Ground Zero. And it wasn't just any bunch of lawyers. It was Cadwalader, Wickersham & Taft, founded nearby in 1792; it is the oldest continuously practicing law firm in America. Cadwalader *is* Lower Manhattan. It wasn't just any space, either. Those 14 floors were to have been among those occupied by Lehman Brothers. Instead, the financial giant headed uptown to the Times Square district where it bought a building. It also took space on Park Avenue. Cadwalader's decision to take Lehman's rejected high floor space, despite attractive alternatives in midtown, was the most potent signal yet that the bloodied neighborhood has not only survived but is once again a desirable setting for top-end businesses.

In representing Cadwalader, Studley faced the kind of complications on which it thrives. For starters, this was not just a case of tenant versus owner (Brookfield Properties), but also tenant versus Lehman Brothers, the primary leaseholder. Cadwalader was loathe to sublet from Lehman Brothers. What if Lehman were to suffer reverses and fail to pay its rent to Brookfield? This could create problems for Cadwalader. In prolonged three-way negotiations, Studley won for its client a direct 20-year lease at a lower rental than Lehman had been paying. It also got concessions from the city to keep Cadwalader downtown. Anticipating future growth, the law firm also secured an option on an additional 400,000 square feet at One World Financial Center.

That negotiation was fairly standard stuff for Studley. Less so was Studley's handling of a unique eventuality: One day, up-close construction will start on the Freedom Tower expected to rise 1776 feet from the footprint of the great destruction. Would the din make Cadwalader's working conditions intolerable? To find out, Studley hired acoustic engineers who figured out how many decibels of noise would be individually produced by an array of construction equipment including piledrivers, jackhammers, cement mixers, and giant bulldozers. The engineers had to calculate how much of that noise would be attenuated by the curtain wall facade of Cadwalader's upper floor offices.

The bottom line of the study was that the noise would be tolerable for Cadwalader's staff. But all parties involved understood that the disruption had its symbolic upside. Those decibels, as well as the dirt and dust outside Cadwalader's east-facing windows, will represent Lower Manhattan resurrected. Call it the good noise.

Sources

My main source of material has been interviews with persons connected to Studley and its founder, done over four years and compiled into notes totaling over 60,000 words. Supplemental information about the company came from *Studley Ink*, a newsletter published by Julien J. Studley Inc. from 1987 to 1996.

Where I have quoted from or relied on information in a newspaper, magazine, or book to fill in details in the narrative, references are incorporated into the text.

Chapter 5, "Assemblage," originally appeared in *New York Magazine* ("How They Assembled the Most Expensive Block in New York's History," February 25, 1974). A number of conversations in the story were recreated based on the recollections of interviewees.

For particulars about New York locations, I relied on the following:

Brockmann, Jorg, and Harris, Bill. *One Thousand New York Buildings.* New York: Black Dog & Leventhal Publishers, 2002.

Jackson, Kenneth T., ed. *The Encyclopedia of New York City.* New Haven: Yale University Press, and New York: The New-York Historical Society, 1995.

Stern, Robert A.M., Mellins, Thomas, and Fishman, David. *New York 1960: Architecture and Urbanism Between the Second World War and the Bicentennial.* 2nd ed. New York: The Monacelli Press, 1997.

White, Norval, and Willensky, Elliot. *AIA Guide to New York City.* 4th ed. New York: Three Rivers Press, 2000.

Yale Robbins, Inc. *Office Buildings.* Editions from November 1994 and Winter 2001–2002.

Index